Stumpers!

Stumpers!

Answers to Hundreds of Questions That Stumped the Experts

EDITED BY

Fred R. Shapiro

RANDOM HOUSE   NEW YORK

Stumpers! by Fred R. Shapiro

Copyright © 1998 by Random House, Inc.

Library of Congress Cataloging-in-Publication Data

Stumpers! : answers to hundreds of questions that stumped the experts
/ [compiled by] Fred Shapiro.
    p.   cm.
    Includes index.
    ISBN 0-375-70174-5
    1. Questions and answers.   I. Shapiro, Fred R.   II. Stumpers.
AG195.S78   1998
031.02—dc21   98-21568
                                           CIP

Visit the Random House Web site at www.randomhouse.com

Typeset and printed in the United States of America.

1998 First Edition

0 9 8 7 6 5 4 3 2
September 1998
ISBN 0-375-70174-5

New York   Toronto   London   Sydney   Auckland

Contents

Preface

Imagine a machine to which you could submit any question, on any subject from sports to music to history to science, and receive an authoritative answer within hours, sometimes minutes. Imagine that this Answer Machine was more powerful than any reference book or any database or any World Wide Web search engine, because it combined the abilities of many researchers, each of whom brought extensive information-finding experience and collections of book and electronic information-finding tools to the task of responding to your question. This is the concept of Stumpers, one of the most remarkable resources on the Internet, and this book is a collection of some of the "greatest hits" of Stumpers questions and answers.

Stumpers was created in 1992 by Anne Feeney, a student at the Graduate School of Library and Information Science at Rosary College (now Dominican University) in Illinois. Feeney later wrote, "As an undergraduate at Carleton College, I had discovered that I could use the Internet to contact experts . . . in nearly any field, most of whom were delighted to share information and speculation on all kinds of topics. I often thought that a formal, organized network of such experts would be a wonderful research tool." So she initiated an Internet e-mail discussion list, using the Mailserv software, named Stumpers (the name was suggested by Michael Koenig, dean of the Rosary library school at that time). This discussion list allows participants to post questions to the thousand or so subscribers, some of whom will then post answers that are in turn sent to the subscribers on the list. The list continues to be maintained by the Dominican University Graduate School of Library and Information Science and moderated by students at that school.

The "Welcome to Stumpers-List" message describes Stumpers as "a networking resource for reference questions that have people, in essence, stumped. It is assumed that all questions posted to this list have been thoroughly researched through the usual sources: library, specialists, other Internet resources, etc." Another ground rule is that the list should remain focused on questions and answers rather than discursive discussions (although humor in questions and answers is acceptable and indeed welcomed!). The "Welcome" message further specifies: "Please cite the source of your answer."

Although most subscribers are librarians, Stumpers is emphatically not restricted to librarians: professors, students, editors, lawyers, computer geeks, and just plain ordinary folks with inquiring minds can all be found as active participants or quiet lurkers. The nonlibrarians sometimes contribute an expertise in a particular field that supplements the general wizardry of the trained reference librarians. The scope of the human resources networked by Stumpers is also broad geographically: Subscribers hail not only from virtually every state of the United States but also from Canada, Great Britain, Norway, Denmark, South Africa, Israel, Australia, New Zealand, and other countries around the world.

Stumpers does have its shortcomings, and can fall short of the ideal of the Answer Machine in a number of respects. Traffic is heavy, and some of the posters disregard Stumpers guidelines, posing questions that could be answered by basic reference works or engaging in conjecture or extraneous ramblings rather than providing solid answers to queries. Many members of the list are librarians in small public libraries without the resources to solve the really tough reference riddles; more involvement by librarians at large research libraries would make for an even more powerful network.

These weaknesses, however, may actually be strengths. Because public library reference desks tend to receive the questions that are most on the minds of the general populace, the predominance of public libraries on Stumpers ensures that virtually all of the most popular mysteries and fascinations of our age pop up on the list at one time or another. The give-and-take, even the digressions, of Stumpers postings can create a rich conversation beyond the dry basics of questions and responses, and can inspire further research that adds depth to the original answer.

Whatever the precise chemistry underlying Stumpers may be, the end result is a resource that stands out dramatically from the mass of chatter that characterizes the Internet. The librarian's role represents centuries of effort devoted to collecting, evaluating, organizing, and providing access to knowledge. The Internet in many ways has thrown out the wisdom of these centuries and started over with billions of bytes of raw, unevaluated, unreliable, unorganized, difficult-to-access information. For every valuable Internet nugget, there are a hundred or a thousand specimens of banality, error, or bigotry. Stumpers questions and answers, preserved in the online Stumpers Archives, are one of the major repositories of accurate information on the Net. As we make the epochal transition from the book culture of the past to the brave new online world, Stumpers may be viewed as preserving the librarian's virtues of responsiveness, reliability, and accuracy in a digital environment sorely in need of precisely those qualities.

In the present book I have collected many of the finest gems of Stumpers questions and answers to provide pleasure and information to readers. My criteria in selecting these "threads" of queries and responses have been informativeness, entertainment value, and broad interest. The compilation is of course subjective and incomplete. Another editor would doubtless have chosen different items. Stumpers contributions that may be beloved by the list's aficionados, such as the marvelous poems of the erudite and witty John Dyson, a professor of Spanish and Portuguese at Indiana University, have been left out because they are either not of broad enough interest or not truly responsive to a question. A disproportionate number of my own postings are here, not because of my unbridled ego (although that may be part of it), but because I tend more than others on the list to "cut to the chase" and provide authoritative answers with a minimum of accompanying "noise."

I have included some of the most compelling puzzles, those that come to reference librarians repeatedly because thousands of people are wondering about them, as well as quirkier but intriguing topics. The range of subjects encompassed is as wide as human curiosity: entertainment, sports and games, urban legends and folklore, language, literature, music, art, religion, people, history, geography, government and law, crime and punishment, the military, the body, animals, science, and technology and communications are only some of the categories.

The questions and answers themselves are presented for the most part as they were posted on Stumpers. They have been lightly edited for consistency and readability, and some extraneous parts of messages have been deleted. Much of the apparatus of e-mail, such as headers, has been omitted so that the messages read easily in book format. For example, titles of books or movies that had the form _Legends of the Fall_ in the original posting have been altered to the conventional printed style, *Legends of the Fall*. The individual who posted the question and answer is identified in the way he or she wished to be, except that in a few instances where it was not possible to reach the author of a question to obtain his or her permission for reprinting, the question has been paraphrased without identifying an author.

Within topical categories such as "Crime and Punishment," each thread of question and answers is grouped under a heading ("Fateful Vehicle," "Female Assassination Victims," etc.). Questions are identified with a **Q,** answers with an **A.** Often, more than one answer is printed. A subject index and an index of authors of messages appear at the end of the book.

Glossary of Terms

Although I have edited the entries in this book to minimize the use of esoteric terms, references, and abbreviations, some recurring terms may be unfamiliar to nonlibrarians or to those new to Stumpers. The more important of these are explained below:

Archives All messages on the Stumpers lists back to 1993 are archived. Old messages on a particular topic can be found by searching by keyword. Messages from a particular year and month can also be retrieved. To access the Stumpers Archives, you can point your World Wide Web browser at the URL http://www.cuis.edu/~stumpers/intro.html (the official Web pages) or http://www.du.edu/~penrosel/wombat/ (the unofficial Web pages maintained by T. F. Mills of the University of Denver Library, one of the major contributors to Stumpers). You can also use a gopher command (gopher gopher.cuis.edu) to access the Archives.

Nexis A database containing the full text of millions of newspaper and magazine articles and wire service stories.

The Oxford English Dictionary (OED) The OED is the most comprehensive dictionary of the English language, and it attempts to trace each word and phrase included back to its earliest appearance in print.

Patron The "customer" of a library. Most of the questions in this book were initiated when a library patron asked a reference librarian for help with a query.

Wombat The mascot of Stumpers. See Lois Fundis's Foreword, "Why an Obscure Marsupial Became an Amusing Tradition."

How to Subscribe to Stumpers

If you enjoy this book and would like to subscribe to the Stumpers list, do not send your request to the list itself. Rather, send an e-mail message to the following address:

MAILSERV@CRF.CUIS.EDU

The body of the message should be the following:

SUBSCRIBE STUMPERS-L

MAILSERV will respond with an automatically generated message.

Foreword

Why an Obscure Marsupial Became an Amusing Tradition

Why has a furry burrowing marsupial
Obscure to many non-Stumpers-List members
Mushroomed from a routine reference question,
Ballooned into a long-running joke,
And—despite controversy—hung on with its sharp claws
To triumphantly reign as our mailing-list's mascot?

Before May 1994, only one wombat appears in the Stumpers Archives, and that was someone's e-mail address. The situation changed rapidly, however, when someone posted a message on May 17, "Looking for the name of a baby wombat." This was the entire message and the person signed only her e-mail address. She has since come forward as Alicia Bell, children's librarian at the Framingham Public Library in Massachusetts. "We had no idea our small question would become such a huge part of Internet lore," she notes.

Dennis Lien, being a reference librarian and thus eager to help, thought at first that the person wanted to name a pet, then that they might be looking for a wombat character from fiction (children's lit? SF?), and finally realized they wanted the generic term for the young of wombats (as *kitten* is for cats). These tries were posted as three separate answers that afternoon; the second and third ones were about a half-hour apart.

Just about that time—roughly 5:30 P.M. EDT—there was a computer glitch of, if not epic proportions, then at least epic significance to Stumpers. Somehow the computer at Concordia University Information Systems (the CUIS of our mailserv-list and gopher addresses) in River Forest, Illinois, got caught in a loop with another computer. This caused messages sent out at that time to be repeated over and over and over and . . .

Fortunately the list was a bit slow that day. Other than Dennis's last two messages about baby wombats, there was one on "witches' walks" (aka widows' walks). By actual count the two wombat messages from Dennis are in the archives five and eleven times. (The "witches" one is in there even more times.) List lore, from the memories of those who were on the receiving end of these endlessly looped messages, claim that this is a low number, that it was dozens of times, maybe fifty or more! I cannot explain this discrepancy, but by the morning of May 18 everyone's mailbox was full of witches and wombats. And here's where the fun begins.

With characteristic Stumpers humor, Dennis began making light of the situation. Signing off messages later that week, he either reassured everybody, "The above has nothing to do with wombats. Honest" or else asked, "So, hey, have I told you all lately about wombats . . . ARGH! No! Don't hit!"

Had the people involved in the witches'/widows' walks question had a similar sense of humor about it, the history of this list would be much different, but apparently they decided to keep mum. Meanwhile Dennis kept on with the wombat lines: "If you love wombats, set them free. Otherwise people will talk" and (because the "If you love someone" quote may have come from Frederick S. Perls) "Wombats do not concern themselves with seeking out perls of wisdom" (May 22 and May 23, respectively).

More wombatty remarks ensued, with other people joining in the fun (on May 24, Dennis Clark added to a message about how someone had died, "Just my entry in this game of Mortal Wombat.") as well as with more facts about real (furry) wombats, including some confirming Dennis's statement that the term requested for a baby wombat is most likely *joey*—Australian for babies of all species, including homo sapiens. If you look in the archives you will find that there have been other suggestions, but *joey* is the best documented. (My favorite, however, is *wombaby*.)

Some people pointed out that about this same time *Witch and Wombat,* a children's book by Carolyn Cushman, was published. As part of the wombatmania, excerpts from the book were posted to the list. Why it didn't win the Newbery we'll never know! Other wombat facts that have surfaced include a school mascot (a University of Wisconsin branch campus—the main campus mascot being a badger), a women's bicycling group, a computer information database and even a Web site devoted to real, furry marsupial wombats.

One of the all-time classics of Stumpers history came on June 7 when Dennis Lien answered a question about a saddlemaker named

Gallatin in cowboy lingo that would've made Gabby Hayes proud. He closed with "Happy trails, and keep your library paste dry," signed it "Dennis 'The Minnesota Kid' Lien . . ." and concluded with "Reckon you must be the new wombat in town, ma'm?" It would be worth learning to use the Archives to find this alone (try keyword searching under *saddles*)—unless, of course, you don't like to laugh in the library.

On June 9—just a little more than three weeks after the baby-wombat question—Rob Groman of the Amarillo Public Library in Texas made not one but two highly prescient remarks after his signature:

> (Someday, some unsuspecting librarian will go into the Stumpers-l archives to look for information on wombats, . . . and won't they be surprised. Will the wombat become the official mascot of the stumpers list?)

By July there were about sixty wombat comments or jokes in addition to the original May 17 messages. Wombatmania had taken hold. When John Henderson wondered why no one had objected, a flame war burst out, referred to by some as the Great Wombat War: Some people thought the wombattery was a "waste of money, brains and time," but others were of the "all work and no play" school, regarding it as an innocent way to let off steam—and of course no one was being forced to make wombat jokes.

Even by this time there had already been some questions about how the wombat thing got started. "You had to be there" was a common response. Susan L. Benzer added (July 11), "It was just a spread of mass hysteria with the mere mention of the W word to get us poor victims hysterical all over again." (Referring to the saddle answer, ". . . I keep seeing the wombat in a ten-gallon hat with six-guns . . .")

Also, since the American Library Association held its annual conference in late June, there was a discussion of a "Wombat Gathering in Miami" so that people could meet each other face to face (Sue Kamm's proposal of this on June 14 seems to be the first message in which *wombat* referred to the human members of the list). Wombat T-shirts and buttons were proposed and designed. So much list time was taken up with discussions of the design that Kirsten Almstead suggested a "mini-mailserv . . . solely devoted to Wombat T-s? (Kind of a wombat-lane of the info. hwy.)"

Since the Great Wombat War, the frequency of wombat jokes has died down somewhat. A recent search of the archives (WARNING: this takes up beaucoup megabytes and a LOT of time!!!!) shows far fewer per month than during the June/July 1994 peak. Partly, though, this is due to the development of wombat Netiquette: because the words *wombat* and *wombats* occur so frequently in the archives, many longtime list members refrain from using the "W word." Instead they spell it "w★mb★t" or "w----t" or use other circumlocutions, such as "the furry critter" or "the animal that dare not speak its name." Since you can't search by symbols in the archives, there is no way to find "w★mb★t" jokes. This makes it hard to collect them, but it keeps the Archives from being utterly overwhelmed with wombat references.

Digression on natural history of wombats followeth:

Another circumlocution is by using various forms of the scientific names of the wombat: Vombatidae or Phascolomyidae (which are two different family names for the same family; sources vary) or the genus names Vombatus, Phascolomis, or Lasiorhinus—Vombatus ursinus, or Phascolomis ursinus, depending on your source, being the common wombat. The hairy-nosed wombat, sometimes called the soft-furred wombat, is Lasiorhinus latifrons. Phascolomis or Phascolomyidae, by the way, means "pouched mouse" (Greek *phaskolon,* pouch + *mys,* mouse). "Vombat" comes from "wombat"—*v* being pronounced as *w* in Latin—which in turn comes from aboriginal Australian languages. They're pretty big "mice"; my sources say adult wombats are "woodchuck-like" and approximately 1 to 1.6 meters long, weighing 18 to 36 kg (3 to 4 feet and 40 to 80 pounds to some of us).

David Bugler from Queensland, where they know about such things, comments, "We phascolomyophiles much prefer to spread the word that woodchucks are in fact wombat-like (though without the Churchillian charisma of a heavy, slow-moving wombat)."

Bears, too, resemble wombats. Indeed, the "ursinus" in the species name means "bear" or "bear-like," and Chana Lajcher has passed along the information that the Hebrew name for the wombat, *dubon ha-kees,* means "pocket teddy bear." Since wombats are cousins of the koala, this seems highly appropriate.

Wombats were also known as badgers (cf. the Wisconsin teams mentioned above) by European settlers who (aaugh! cannibalism!) enjoyed "badger ham." This probably relates to the wombat's proclivity for burrowing. Grzimek's *Encyclopedia of Mammals* tells the story of wombats who escaped from a zoo until the zookeepers put a concrete floor in the animals' cage.

Did you know that fossil wombats were discovered by scientists before they had seen the living ones? Did you know that the largest of all marsupials was a member of the Superfamily Vombatoidea (which also includes koalas and "diprotodonts," a fossil family)—this was the *Diprotodon optatum,* which the *Encyclopedia Britannica* says "was built something like a huge ground sloth and attained the size of a large rhinoceros." It existed in the late Pleistocene. Then there was "the giant wombat, *Phascolonus gigas,* which was as large as a black bear . . ." It also lived during the Pleistocene.

Digression on natural history endeth.

Our Stumpers wombat does not have a name. On December 15, 1994, T. F. Mills noted "We have a mascot (Wombat), a god (Sirilius), and now I think we have a king. Charles keeps raising his head." I have since noted that by this same logic we also have a comedy troupe: Monty Python (who would no doubt name the wombat Bruce).

Meanwhile, back at the ranch, on February 20, 1995, Bill Lowe suggested dropping the wombat in favor of Sirilius as resident in-joke; the next day David Lundquist suggested that instead Sirilius should be the name of the wombat. Other suggestions have been Joey, Willie—a Willie or Willy Wombat appears occasionally as a foil of the Tazmanian Devil of Looney Tunes fame—and recently Dewey. But the poor phascolomid is still anonymous.

While on vacation I saw one of the Taz/Willie Wombat toons. Taz had provoked Willie to the point that his next logical (in Looney Tunes logic, that is) response would be the line, "I suppose you know this means war!" But Willie refused to do a cheap Bugs Bunny imitation. So in revenge the writers/artists dropped Willie and Taz into other Looney Tunes settings: Coyote and Road Runner, Sylvester and Tweety, Fog—ah, say Foghorn Leghorn and the dog, Snuffy. In each segment, Taz was the bird, which means, natch, that the wombat was still the foil. (Does Warners have an antimammalian bias?) Dressed as Tweety in a (tight) yellow-feathered costume and crammed into the tiny bird cage, Taz says, "I tot I taw a puddy wombat! I did! I did!"

(Oh, the research I did for this!!!!)

I have been trying to collect some of the Wombat Words of Wisdom that have appeared on the list (a huge task, and I'm sure I'll never get them all, not even counting the nonwombat humor). Those mentioned above are merely a sample. Someday, I don't know when, I will get it all typed into the computer. I'll just leave you with one more for now:

> As wombats cruise down the Information Highway, they think it's important to take time off to stop and eat the flowers.
> —Dennis Lien, July 27, 1994

Lois Aleta Fundis
Reference Librarian
Mary H. Weir Public Library
Weirton, WV

Stumpers!

Mr. Gilligan

 Well, I haven't had much luck getting any of my questions answered this week, but I bet you all know this one (even though I don't). Patron said he can get three hours off work if he can come up with Gilligan's first name (from the TV show *Gilligan's Island*).

We've gone into the Stumper's Archives and the two Web sites with no luck. I have no books here that have been able to help us. Is Gilligan his first or last name?

Susan Behring
Reference Librarian
Brigham City Library
Brigham City, UT

Two days ago, I heard the producer of *Gilligan's Island*, Jack Arnold, being interviewed on a Chicago radio station. He was asked what Gilligan's first name was.

His response:

Gilligan *never* had a first name on the show.

After the show was out of production and into reruns, Arnold and the actor who played Gilligan [Bob Denver] were having lunch.

The actor said Gilligan deserved a first name.

So the producer said *if* Gilligan had had a first name, he would have had the name Willie.

Mona Mosho
Information Services Librarian
Joliet Public Library
Joliet, IL

□ □ □

Whoa, Horse

 I have had a request to locate the name of Dudley Do-Right's horse. Anybody out there know this?

Dawn Zeh
Researcher
Microsoft Library
Redmond, WA

 The name of the cartoon character Dudley Do-Right's horse has been covered in the past, but scanning the responses in Stumper's Archives I've found the wrong answer reported. People have cited the first edition of Alec McNeil's work *Total Television* (1973) and given the name "Steed," but that is wrong. The proper name of Dudley Do-Right's horse is Horse.

McNeil's second edition of *Total Television* (1984) acknowledges his error in his revised introduction, and gives the name "Horse"; his third edition also reports this.

The authorized Bullwinkle & Rocky Role-Playing Game from TSR (1988) has an entire chapter of biographical sketches for the show's characters; Horse is included, under the name "Horse" (he's also reported as having been played in the series by Sid Gould's father).

The Dudley Do-Right Gift Emporium in Hollywood, founded by Jay Ward and run by his widow, sells assorted paraphernalia related to the show, including various items portraying Horse, and using that name.

Of the twelve videocassettes of the assorted cartoon shows released by Buena Vista (*Rocky & Bullwinkle, Dudley Do-Right,* and *The Bullwinkle Show*), none refers to the horse as anything but Horse (Dudley does call him "faithful steed" once, but as an honorific, not a name).

Other sources such as George Woolery's *Children's Television: The First Thirty-Five Years, 1946–1981*, still "the classic," also report Horse as "Horse."

Greg Kelley
Public Services Librarian
St. Paul Public Library
St. Paul, MN

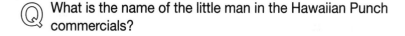

Punch Drunk

 What is the name of the little man in the Hawaiian Punch commercials?

The character who went around asking if anyone wanted a good Hawaiian Punch was Punchy. His victim's name was Oaf.

I got this information from a Lexis/Nexis search I did earlier today.

Ross Martin, later of *The Wild, Wild West* fame, was the original voice of Punchy. He was succeeded by Len Maxwell, who specialized in voice-overs and cartoon voices. When Punchy was revived after a hiatus of about fifteen years, Maxwell sued the makers of Hawaiian Punch, asserting that he had proprietary rights to the characterization. He lost the suit.

Jim Hunt
Associate Professor
Business and Online Search Specialist
University Library
California State University
Dominguez Hills, CA

Ozzie and Harriet Break Down the Barriers

Q We would like to know the first TV couple that was allowed to sleep in the same bed. My colleague checked many sources and couldn't find the answer. I checked the Archives (being a good little wombat) under a variety of search terms, and found nothing. I was surprised that a question of this magnitude had not been asked by some of our thirsty-for-knowledge patrons. We know that Rob and Laura slept in separate beds, but Carol and Mike Brady were snuggly at the end of each episode. I always thought it was kinky, well never mind that now!

If anyone out there can name the couple and the show, we would appreciate it. Actually now that I think on it, Darrin and Samantha got to sleep together, why not Rob and Laura? Weren't they contemporaries?

Marijo Kist
Glendale, AZ

A I came across a posting by Marijo Kist in 1995 asking who were the first TV couple allowed to sleep in the same bed. There was never a documented answer, but the most popular choice among respondents was Herman and Lily Munster. (Other suggestions were Carol and Mike Brady of *The Brady Bunch,* Lucy and Ricky Ricardo in one of the later episodes of *I Love Lucy,* Wilma and Fred Flintstone of The Flintstones, and Luke and his wife from *The Real McCoys.*)

No one mentioned Ozzie and Harriet Nelson of *Ozzie and Harriet,* but this may be the correct answer. I found in a Nexis search that the *New York Times,* January 19, 1997, noted that "Ozzie frequently bragged that he and Harriet were the first couple in a television series to be shown sleeping in the same bed." According to a letter in the *Houston Chronicle* of August 18, 1996, the Trivial Pursuit game has Ozzie and Harriet as the answer for this question. From an AltaVista search, I also found that the FAQ file for the alt.tv.brady-bunch newsgroup says that Ozzie and Harriet were the first same-bed TV couple.

Fred R. Shapiro
Associate Librarian for Public Services
Yale Law School
New Haven, CT

□ □ □

The End of Alfalfa

 I have a patron who is looking for the name of the actor who played Alfalfa in *The Little Rascals*.

I have looked in many TV books here, and hardly any of them even mention *The Little Rascals* or the *Our Gang* series.

Terry Wirick
Information Services Librarian
Erie County Public Library
Erie, PA

Alfalfa's real name was Carl Switzer and, in a fun bit of trivia, he can be seen, grown-up, in *It's a Wonderful Life* as one of the boys who pulls the switch at the high school gym that throws everyone into the swimming pool.

Alfalfa was killed in a dispute over some money back in the 1950s, I believe; his last words were (no kidding), "I want that fifty dollars you owe me, and I want it now!"

Sally G. Waters
Queen of Reference
Stetson College of Law Library
St. Petersburg, FL

I met Carl Switzer when I was in the third grade in Hutchinson, Kansas, where he resided. For what it is worth, the local newspapers reported that he killed himself accidentally while cleaning a gun.

Michael Moulds
Adult Services Manager
Glenside Public Library District
Glendale Heights, IL

 Carl Switzer was shot to death in 1959. Source: *Our Gang* by Leonard Maltin.

Chuck Cody
Reference Librarian
Columbus Metropolitan Library
Columbus, OH

□ □ □

Slowly I Turn . . .

 A friend librarian from across the state needs the completion of a quote that contains the following words:

> *Slowly I turn, step by step, inch by inch*

or it may be reversed:

> *Slowly I turn, inch by inch, step by step*

She thinks it may have come from a Three Stooges film or an Abbott and Costello film.

We're not sure of our sources, but our library doesn't have any quotation books, and she has heard me rave about how great the Stumpers list is for finding references, so she called me for a favor.

Stephanie McKinnon
Harris Corporation Library
Melbourne, FL

It's an old vaudeville routine, and in more modern times it was on an *I Love Lucy* episode (#19) shown on 2-18-52 (from *The I Love Lucy Book* by Bart Andrews).

Roger Mendel
Alpena County Library
Alpena, MI

 Saw Abbott and Costello's *Lost in a Harem* (MGM, 1944) this past Sunday, and it did have a version of the routine.

A & C are in a jail cell with the Derelict (Murray Leonard). The Derelict tells them his tale of woe, how he took a poor stranger into his home and how the stranger ran off with the Derelict's wife and baby son. He eventually caught up with the dastard "on the banks of the Pokomoko" (Pokomoko is the trigger in this version).

The Derelict: . . . . slo-o-o-o-wly I turned. Step by step, step by step I crept up on him, and when I saw the sneer on his face I struck! And I grabbed him [grabs Lou], and I [becomes unintelligible, shakes Lou around, then lets him go, laughing maniacally].

Bill Thomas
Reference Librarian
County of Los Angeles Public Library
Lancaster, CA

 I must admit to knowing one of the sources for this. It was from a very old Three Stooges routine that probably originated in vaudeville. It was a skit about a semi-deranged man (Moe) whose lover was stolen by an alleged friend. Whenever he heard the words "Niagara Falls," he began to recite the litany "inch by inch, step by step" and proceeded to stalk the nearest male and assault him (it was always Larry or Curly). To find the exact title of the sketch, I would recommend trying a film book about the Three Stooges.

Montgomery Phair
Reference Librarian
Baltimore County Public Library
Randallstown, MD

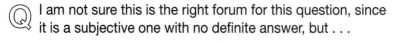

The Scandalous Ten

 I am not sure this is the right forum for this question, since it is a subjective one with no definite answer, but . . .

. . . what would be considered the ten greatest Hollywood scandals? The patron is open-minded about what he allows as a scandal (Would you consider the blacklisting of the Hollywood Ten a scandal? Sure. How about the *Heaven's Gate* fiasco? Well, OK), but I think he would prefer good old-fashioned sex scandals like Fatty Arbuckle's lurid trial for rape and murder (even if poor Fatty was innocent).

Personal lists would be fine, but citations of books compiled on that subject would also be useful.

John Henderson
Reference Librarian
Ithaca College Library
Ithaca, NY

What a lovely, juicy question for a Friday afternoon! Doubtless there will be other suggestions but I would recommend the following:

First of all, Kenneth Anger's classics, *Hollywood Babylon* and *Hollywood Babylon II*. Virtually no Hollywood sex scandal is left unexamined, it has a feast of bizarre photos, and he is positively libelous in his prose.

The People's Almanac 2 by David Wallechinski and Irving Wallace offers a section called "Historic Hollywood Scandals" (pp. 755–762), which gives short profiles on the Arbuckle trial, the death of Thomas Ince, Mary Astor's diary, Joan Berry's paternity suit against Charlie Chaplin, and Ingrid Bergman's affair with Roberto Rossellini. The Wallace-Wallechinski duo also wrote a book called *The Intimate Sex Lives of Famous People,* which includes many Hollywood stars as well.

Some titles dealing with individual scandals include the following:

Samuel Marx, *Deadly Illusions.* (This deals with the death of Jean Harlow's husband Paul Bern. Marx, an MGM insider, alleges that Bern was murdered by his common-law wife.)

Andy Edmonds, *Hot Toddy.* (Biography of Thelma Todd, which sheds new light on her mysterious death.)

Sidney Kirkpatrick, *A Cast of Killers.* (The murder of William Desmond Taylor, as solved by King Vidor.)

Two books are available about Fatty Arbuckle: David Yallop, *The Day the Laughter Stopped,* and Andy Edmonds, *Frame-Up!*

And finally, there are some stars whose sex lives were so active that their biographies merit mention here:

Errol Flynn, *My Wicked, Wicked Ways.* (Witty and colorful, this includes Flynn's own account of his rape trials.) Another interesting account of Flynn's personal life is found in Florence Aadland's *The Big Love* (recently reissued in paperback with a foreword by William Styron), which is the story of her teenaged daughter Beverly, who was Flynn's last mistress.

David Stenn, *Clara Bow: Runnin' Wild.* (No, contrary to legend, she didn't take on the entire USC football team, but she had affairs with such persons as Victor Fleming, Gary Cooper, Bela Lugosi, and John Gilbert [among others], had to pay out $25,000 to avoid being named as corespondent in a divorce suit, and brought charges against her secretary for embezzlement [the secretary retaliated by spilling the dirt on Clara's sex life]—all of which makes some juicy reading.)

Maria Riva, *Marlene Dietrich.* (Riva, Dietrich's daughter, names many of the lovers both male and female; but others have tantalizing code names, and it's fun to try to figure them out. Unless I've guessed wrong, it looks as if she slept with almost everybody of note from the first half of the twentieth century except FDR, Hitler, Bogart, and Garbo.)

Floyd Conner, *Lupe Velez and Her Lovers.* (Regrettably, this book seems to have been composed almost entirely from secondary sources, so there's more on the lovers than on Lupe. But with an assortment that included Johnny Weismuller, Gary Cooper, Douglas Fairbanks, Sr., Charlie Chaplin, Jack Johnson, and John Gilbert, one realizes that the Mexican Spitfire must have been a pretty spicy dish; Errol Flynn wrote in *My Wicked, Wicked Ways* that he knew from personal experience that she was able to rotate her left breast clockwise.)

At any rate, this is enough of a reading list to get you started.

Denise Montgomery
Information Services Librarian
Odum Library
Valdosta State University
Valdosta, GA

□ □ □

Archaeology of the Sequel

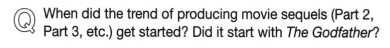 When did the trend of producing movie sequels (Part 2, Part 3, etc.) get started? Did it start with *The Godfather*?

What about the wonderful ol' cliff-hanger serials of the thirties and forties (*Buck Rogers, Superman,* etc.)? I guess it would depend on how one defines the word *sequel*. Also, I believe there were more than one of the old soundless movies with Mighty Joe Young.

David Merchant
University of Tennessee
School of Information Science
Knoxville, TN

As I'd define the word *sequel,* we have to go back at least as far as Valentino's silent films: *The Sheik* (1922) and *Son of the Sheik* (1926).

According to *Film Index International,* the official titles of the *Godfather* sequelae were *The Godfather,* Part 2, and *The Godfather,* Part 3, rather than *Godfather II* and *Godfather III* as they were frequently billed. Since *Godfather II* officially isn't entitled to the numeral, *Jaws II* (1977) wins out over *Exorcist II* (1978), at least according to *FII.*

Gary Lee Phillips
Computer Services Librarian
Columbia College
Chicago, IL

 I guess it would depend on one's definition of sequels. The numbering parts probably did start with *Godfather,* etc., but counting films that have continuing characters and themes . . . well, that would go way back into the thirties, forties, and fifties—even the twenties, if you count Rudy's sheiks or Chaplin's tramp. But sequels and series have been popular for a long time. In the thirties and forties there were *The Thin Man* and its sequels (Nick and Nora Charles); Hopalong Cassidy (sixty-six films from the original Hopalong Cassidy!); the Andy Hardy series; Boston Blackie; Sherlock Holmes (with Basil Rathbone); Ma and Pa Kettle; Charlie Chan; Tarzan; and Francis the Talking Mule. Beginning in the sixties, of course, came James Bond. To name a few!

Some of you youngsters probably don't know what the heck all of those were . . . but they were certainly continuing sequels.

Chuck Billodeaux
Community Library Manager
Lancaster Public Library—City of Los Angeles
Lancaster, CA

The Grand Slam of Entertainment

 The Bay Area Library and Information System has done lots of legwork to provide the answer to the question of which individuals have won the Grand Slam of entertainment (the Grammy, Emmy, Oscar, and Tony awards).

Since the answer wasn't found in any standard reference work, I am sharing it with the Stumpers Archives for posterity: Rita Moreno, Julie Andrews, Sir John Gielgud, Helen Hayes, Audrey Hepburn, Marvin Hamlisch, and Peter Ustinov. As far as we now know, Rita Moreno is the only one to have received the Grammy, Emmy, Oscar, Tony (Grand Slam)—and the Golden Globe.

Jamie McGrath
Senior Librarian
Alameda Free Library Reference Department
Alameda, CA

 How about Barbra Streisand?

Grammy—various recordings

Oscar—*Funny Girl* (Best Actress, 1968) and for song-writing

Emmy—for her specials

Tony—? not sure

I seem to recall that Barbra was one of the ones who have all of the major awards, as is Rita Moreno. As for the Golden Globe . . . ?

Donna Hesson
Manager, Lilienfeld Libraries
School of Hygiene and Public Health
Johns Hopkins University
Baltimore, MD

 After checking the facts thoroughly in the Nexis Entertainment Library, I can give definitive answers to some of

the questions that have come up with regard to the Grand Slam of entertainment:

1. Julie Andrews, incredibly, has never won a Tony. In fact she went out of her way to avoid winning a Tony and the Grand Slam in 1996, when she declined a certain Tony for *Victor/Victoria* (certain because she was the only nominee).

2. Barbra Streisand won a Special Award Tony in 1970 as "Best Actress of the Decade." So she is a Grand Slam winner.

3. Rita Moreno is not the only one to win the Grand Slam plus the Golden Globe. Basically, if you've won the Oscar, the Tony, the Emmy, and the Grammy, you've probably won the Golden Globe too. Five of the other Grand Slammers (Streisand, Hamlisch, Ustinov, Audrey Hepburn, and Gielgud) have also won the Golden Globe.

4. Clearly the most impressive award winner is Marvin Hamlisch. He has won not only the Grand Slam plus the Golden Globe, but also the Obie, the Drama Desk Award, and even the Pulitzer Prize! Only the Nobel Prize eludes him.

Fred R. Shapiro
Associate Librarian for Public Services
Yale Law School
New Haven, CT

 Sorry, but Julie Andrews was not the only nominee for that particular Tony award—it was considered a sure thing for her because the other actresses who were also nominated in that category were not quite up to her stature. She had it in a walk! The reason she threw a hissy-fit was that she felt other members of the cast of *Victor/Victoria* had been unfairly ignored by the Tony nominating committee.

Jo Manning
Assistant Professor/Reference Librarian
Otto G. Richter Library
University of Miami
Coral Gables, FL

Here's a correction to my previous Grand Slam of entertainment posting. I was in error about Peter Ustinov being a Grand Slammer; he has never won a Tony.

Fred R. Shapiro
Associate Librarian for Public Services
Yale Law School
New Haven, CT

2 Sports and Games

A Quick Night's Work

Q We have a patron who is looking for the least number of pitches ever thrown in a nine-inning major league baseball game. We have checked numerous baseball encyclopedias and trivia books as well as the Stumpers Archives and the Internet.

Louise Sullivan
Reference Librarian
Spokane Public Library
Spokane, WA

A A Nexis search for the words "fewest pitches" yields many articles, all in agreement as to the record. This mark was set by Charles "Red" Barrett of the Boston Braves on August 10, 1944. In a two-hit shutout of the Reds, Barrett faced only 27 batters and threw only 58 pitches. At 1 hr. 15 min., this was also the shortest night game in history.

Fred R. Shapiro
Associate Librarian for Public Services
Yale Law School
New Haven, CT

□ □ □

Lucky Number

Q Our patron would like to know what famous baseball players wore the number 13 on their jerseys. We already know about Turk Wendell of the Cubs.

We've looked in the Stumpers Archives and every sports almanac and sports trivia and "story of baseball" book we could find, but couldn't find any such list. Does anyone know of one?

Roberta Lincoln
Reference Librarian
Rockford Public Library
Rockford, IL

 Baseball by the Numbers by Mark Stang and Linda Harkness lists players and their numbers team by team.

Among those who have worn #13 are Doyle Alexander (Baltimore Orioles), John Valentin (Boston Red Sox), Lance Parrish (California Angels, Detroit Tigers), Ozzie Guillen (Chicago White Sox), Blue Moon Odom (Oakland Athletics), Dave Concepcion (Cincinnati Reds), Joe Ferguson (Los Angeles Dodgers), Lee Mazzilli (New York Mets), and Roger McDowell (Philadelphia Phillies).

Sue Kamm
Associate Librarian
Inglewood Public Library
Inglewood, CA

□ □ □

The Saddest of Possible Words

Our patron used the phrase "from Tinker to Evers to Chance" in a conversation. The phrase confused the people who heard it. The patron believes that it has to do with a triple play made by those players. I checked *The Baseball Encyclopedia.* I did determine that there were three players—Joe Tinker, Johnny Evers, and Frank Chance—who all played for Chicago at the turn of the century. They were all inducted into the Baseball Hall of Fame in the 1940s. Tinker was a shortstop, Evers played second base, and Chance played first base. Do any base-ball (wom)bats have any ideas?

Pam McLaughlin
Fremont Public Library
Mundelein, IL

These are the saddest of possible words;
"Tinker to Evers to Chance."
Trio of bear cubs, and fleeter than birds,
Tinker and Evers and Chance.
Ruthlessly pricking our gonfalon bubble,
Making a Giant hit into a double,
Words that are weighty with nothing but trouble:
"Tinker to Evers to Chance."

—Franklin Pierce Adams [F.P.A.], "Baseball's Sad Lexicon," quoted in *Bartlett's Familiar Quotations*

Fred R. Shapiro
Associate Librarian for Public Services
Yale Law School
New Haven, CT

They were the first double-play combination to grab the fans' attention. Although the double play is now fairly common, it was a rarity back then until these three fellows honed the art of getting two outs on a grounder to short. The ball would be hit to Tinker, he tossed it to Evers who made the out at second base, and then Evers tossed it to Chance. Obviously, this would only work if there was a man on first, and there were less than two outs when the grounder to short was hit.

Ralph Adam Fine
Judge
Wisconsin Court of Appeals
Milwaukee, WI

[Chance] caught with Chicago until 1902, when manager Frank Selee moved him permanently to first base. The good all-around player remained with Cubs from 1898 to 1912. . . . During the 1905 season, new Cubs owner Charlie W. Murphy appointed Chance player-manager.

—*Biographical Dictionary of American Sports: Baseball* (1987), pp. 83–84

The same book indicates that Tinker to Evers to Chance was "baseball's most celebrated double-play combination" (p. 170).

Two of the three were out of baseball by the time of the Black Sox (World Series fixing) scandal, but Evers was manager of the team from 1913 to 1921 (p. 170), which included the Black Sox year. Unfortunately, according to the same source, Tinker and Evers did not get along off the field. After a quarrel over the payment of a taxicab fare, the two did not speak for nearly three years (p. 557).

John Henderson
Reference Librarian
Ithaca College Library
Ithaca, NY

Damn Yankees

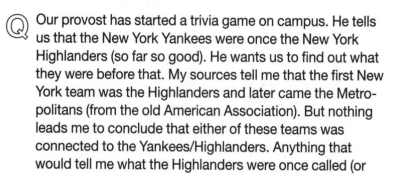

Our provost has started a trivia game on campus. He tells us that the New York Yankees were once the New York Highlanders (so far so good). He wants us to find out what they were before that. My sources tell me that the first New York team was the Highlanders and later came the Metropolitans (from the old American Association). But nothing leads me to conclude that either of these teams was connected to the Yankees/Highlanders. Anything that would tell me what the Highlanders were once called (or that would tell me Highlanders was the original name) would be most useful.

Jimm Wetherbee
Reference/Systems Librarian
E. K. Smith Library
Wingate University
Wingate, NC

 The Baltimore Orioles.

The Baltimore franchise was moribund after playing there in 1901–1902. Frank J. Farrell and Big Bill Devery paid $18,000 for the franchise and moved it to New York. Because it was in the American League, the team seems at first to have been known simply as the New York Americans. Quickly the nickname Highlanders was given to the team, in part because its wooden ballpark called Hilltop Park was built at the point of highest elevation in Manhattan.

Other nicknames included Hilltoppers and Yankees. By 1913, the name Yankees became official.

Sources:

Peter C. Bjarkman, *Encyclopedia of Baseball Team Histories: American League*; Peter Filichia, *Professional Baseball Franchises.*

John Henderson
Reference Librarian
Ithaca College Library
Ithaca, NY

☐ ☐ ☐

Dead Man's Hand

 A patron would like to know the name of a man who was murdered playing poker. The hand he held at the time was named for him. It was recently discussed on a radio talk program and she forgot the man's name.

Sue Prindiville
Head of Reference Services
Naperville Public Libraries
Naperville, IL

 According to *The Gunfighters* by James D. Horan, Wild Bill Hickok was killed on August 2, 1876, by Jack McCall while Hickok was playing poker. He was holding the ace of spades, ace of clubs, two black eights, and the jack of diamonds—since then this hand has been known as "the dead man's hand." McCall killed Hickok because he wanted to be known as a famous gunfighter.

Dianne Brownlee
Reference/Instructional Services Librarian
St. Edward's University Library
Austin, TX

 Here is an authoritative answer from the *Random House Historical Dictionary of American Slang: dead man's hand* . . . a poker hand made up of a pair of eights and a pair of aces, kings, or jacks, with one indifferent card . . . his biographer, Ross, remarks (*Wild Bill,* 298), "The actual cards [held by Hickok] are disputed."

The *RHHDAS*'s earliest recorded citation for the term *dead man's hand,* from the *Century Dictionary Supplement* (1908), specifies the cards as "two pairs, jacks and eights."

Fred R. Shapiro
Associate Librarian for Public Services
Yale Law School
New Haven, CT

Ollie Ollie Oxen Free

 The patron is looking for the origin of a sort of tag in which, when running to the base, the individual calls out "Ollie-Ollie-Olsen-Free." A local reference librarian recalls saying "Ollie-Ollie-All In-Free" when playing hide and seek as a child, but my sources don't verify this saying for the game. I'm sure there are literally hundreds of variations of hide-and-seek. Do any of you Stumpers recall using words to this effect in hide and seek or any other game???

Christine Johnson
Reference Assistant
Northland Library Cooperative
Alpena, MI

 Under the term *olly olly* in *A Dictionary of Catch Phrases,* edited by Paul Beale, there is this entry:

Olly, olly! was, among Cockney schoolchildren of c 1870 to 1920, an invitation to a friend, or a companion, to play a game with, or to accompany, oneself; sometimes a farewell.

Hence, among all Cockneys, a shout of greeting or recognition, usually with a broad, rumbustious, freebooting leer to it.

Perhaps from ho there! Or from the French *allez* (or even both)— rather than the Spanish ole! ole!

In their masterly study *The Lore and Language of School- children* (1959), the Opies list *olly-olly-ee* among a number of terms used to claim a truce or "breather."

Jack Corse
Reference Librarian
Simon Fraser University
Burnaby, British Columbia
Canada

 Here's a good explanation of *ollie ollie oxen free* by Jesse Sheidlower in the April 22, 1997, "Jesse's Word of the Day" feature on the Random House Web site:

Ollie ollie oxen free is one of about a bajillion variants (I know—I counted) of a phrase used in various children's games. As we have seen, children's language and folklore hasn't been as thoroughly studied as one would like, but in this case, researchers have tracked down a huge number of forms.

The phrase is used in a variety of children's chasing games, especially hide-and-(go-)seek. The rough form of this game is that a player (called "it") gives other players a chance to hide, and then tries to find them. When "it" finds the first hider, he calls out some phrase indicating that the other players are "safe" to return "home," at which point the person "it" found will succeed him as "it."

The original form of the phrase was something like *all in free* or *all's out come in free,* both standing for something like *all who are out can come in free.* These phrases got modified to *all-ee all-ee (all) in free* or *all-ee all-ee out(s) in free;* the *-ee* is added, and the *all* is repeated, for audibility and rhythm.

From here the number of variants takes off, and we start seeing folk etymologies in various forms. The most common of these has *oxen* replacing *out(s) in,* giving *all-ee all-ee oxen free;* with the *all-ee* reinterpreted as the name *Ollie,* we arrive at your phrase, which, according to the *Dictionary of American Regional English,* is especially common in California. Norwegian settlement areas have *Ole Ole Olsen's free.* For the *out(s) in* phrase, we also see *ocean, oxford, ax in, awk in,* and even *oops all in.*

This multiplicity of examples demonstrates the unsurprising fact that young children often have little idea what phrases like this mean, and transmute them into variants that involve more familiar terms, losing the original meaning in the process. It's difficult to determine early dates for these expressions—most of them weren't collected until the 1950s and later—but based on recollections of the games, it seems that they were in common use by the 1920s, and probably earlier (*home free* is found in print in the 1890s, and the game hide-and-seek is at least four centuries old).

Fred R. Shapiro
Associate Librarian for Public Services
Yale Law School
New Haven, CT

3 Urban Legends and Folklore

Leave It Under Your Pillow

Q One of our history faculty wants to know the origin of the concept of the tooth fairy. We have checked the *Man and Magic* encyclopedia, various other mythological reference books, general encyclopedias, and the *Oxford English Dictionary*; but while they all tell what the tooth fairy is, they do not tell how this practice got started. Can anybody help? (I have a sneaking suspicion that it may have come about as a public relations ploy on the part of the American Dental Association, but that's just a wild surmise on my part.)

Denise Montgomery
Information Services Librarian
Odum Library
Valdosta State University
Valdosta, GA

A It's not the full answer, but following are several bits that have been sent to "The Exchange" over the years:

A dentist remembered from dental school that St. Apollonia is considered as the tooth fairy. After checking *The Catholic Encyclopedia,* the librarian learned that this saint is popularly invoked against tooth pain, and is represented in art with pincers in which a tooth is held.

On the other hand, two librarians believe that their research indicates a much more recent origin for the tooth fairy. Iona and Peter Opie, in *The Lore and Language of Schoolchildren* (1959), p. 325, describe the legend and then refer to it as a "commercial and apparently modern transaction." A 1928 book by Leo Kanner, *Folklore of the Tooth,* makes no mention of a tooth fairy.

Charles Anderson
Editor, "The Exchange," RQ
(Reference and User Services Quarterly,
a publication of the American Library Association)
Bellevue, WA

In the December 1993 issue of *American Health* magazine, p. 26, a brief paragraph on "tooth fairy economics" states that "the average bounty paid for lost dentition has increased by more than 800 percent during the twentieth century. Talk about inflation's bite!" The article concludes with a table, arranged by decade, of the amount of money the tooth fairy leaves for lost teeth, from 12 cents in 1900–1910 up to $1 in 1993. This is according to Dr. Rosemary Wells, founder and curator of the Tooth Fairy Museum in Deerfield, Illinois. Very interesting!

Judy McMakin
Technical Services Librarian
Richland Public Library
Richland, WA

Maybe we can date the arrival of the tooth fairy on our cultural scene. I'll admit to being sixty, and the tooth fairy gave me a dime for every tooth I put under my pillow in the 1930s in San Francisco!

Dorothy Koenig
Retired Librarian
Berkeley, CA

In *Ethnodentistry and Dental Folklore* (1987) by William J. Carter et al., there is a chapter on "shed tooth rituals" (pp. 72–82). "There are literally hundreds of adages, customs, ceremonies, and prayers that have been associated with the loss of primary teeth" (p. 72). A section on "tooth fairies" (pp. 77–82), suggests that around 1900 in France, Britain, and the United States, the tooth fairy came to replace "more traditional tooth mouse rituals. . . . [T]he recent history of these rituals is poorly documented for all these countries except France." In France, apparently a mouse is still as likely as a fairy to provide the reward.

"The earliest well-documented American tooth fairy ritual dates from 1919, when a source from Utah said a fairy would come in the night and leave a candy bar, penny, nickel, or dime for a lost tooth . . . The word *tooth fairy* probably did not become popular in the United States until 1949, when Lee Rogow published a short story by this name in *Collier's Magazine* (124:126). The first appearance of *tooth fairy* in an encyclopedia was apparently Alan Dundes's article in the 1979 *World Book* . . ."

Ed Morman
Librarian
Institute of the History of Medicine
Johns Hopkins University
Baltimore, MD

□ □ □

The Bare Truth

Q We have a patron who is interested in knowing the name of Lady Godiva's horse. She has visited England and found this information on one of the tours she was on but has forgotten it. We have checked through numerous trivia-type books, the *Imponderables* books, *The Horse's Name Was* . . . , the Stumpers Archives, etc. to no avail. Anyone out there privy to this information? We'd appreciate any leads we can get.

Deb Palmer
Reference Librarian
Cedar Rapids Public Library
Cedar Rapids, IA

It would appear that Lady Godiva's tax-relieving ride through market-crowded Coventry in the eleventh century took place when Coventry was a village with no taxes to relieve and no market to ride through. If one takes the misericord carving in Coventry Cathedral to be the basis for the story, Lady Godiva's horse was a goat. So her "horse's" name was probably Buck or Billy.

John Dyson
Department of Spanish and Portuguese
Indiana University
Bloomington, IN

 Paul Dickson's book, *Names,* apparently gives Aethenoth as the name of Lady Godiva's horse. I get this not from the book itself, but from a review in the *Washington Post,* August 3, 1986, found through a Westlaw/Dialog search. Dickson is a popular, but usually accurate, writer.

Fred R. Shapiro
Associate Librarian for Public Services
Yale Law School
New Haven, CT

 Fred Shapiro's intriguing discovery of the name of Lady Godiva's horse, Aethenoth ("Noble Audacity"), sent me rocketing (well, catapulting, actually) back to Fr. Roger of Wendover, the first to write of this matter in *Flores Historiarum,* if not the last. Alas, the good friar, chronicling scarcely two hundred years after the presumed event (1058 A.D., C.E., Q.E.D.), calls L. G.'s horse *equus,* translating into Latin from the Anglo-Saxon *steda.* I'm not sure what to make of the troubling fact that the lady's palfrey bore two of the same names attributed to Dudley Do-Right's trusty mount.

John Dyson
Department of Spanish and Portuguese
Indiana University
Bloomington, IN

□ □ □

Bad Egg

 What day is the only day of the year you can balance a raw egg on the table, and why is that? We think it's in the month of April.

Dawn Marie Simpson
Marketing Coordinator
Westinghouse Power Generation Business Unit
Orlando, FL

 As nearly as I could tell by searching the Archives, February was the last time we discussed the belief that the only day one can balance an egg (upright, on the broad end) is the day of the vernal equinox. Since this is a recurrent question, I thought it might be good to let everyone know that an authoritative article on the subject was published in the May/June 1996 edition of *Skeptical Inquirer* ("The Great Egg-Balancing Mystery," by Martin Gardner, pp. 8–10).

Gardner discusses the history of the annual egg-balancing ritual, and makes the point that the Chinese, who originated the notion, have a different "first day of spring" than we do (the Chinese one is on or near February 4th, while ours is generally around March 21st). Despite the date discrepancy, members of both cultures believe that eggs will balance only on the day *they* hold to be the first day of spring!

The article also discusses the factors that allow an egg to balance (steady hands, the roughness of the egg's surface, and the roughness of the surface on which the egg is placed) and describes mechanical egg-balancing puzzles and related magician's tricks. Interesting!

Glenn Kersten
Research Librarian
Suburban Library System Reference Service
Oak Park, IL

The notion that an egg can be stood on end only on the vernal equinox is a very old folk myth. I remember at one time seeing an old (probably nineteenth-century) engraving that purported to show Christopher Columbus performing this experiment, supposedly to prove that the world is round (!).

However, if one is patient enough, a hen's egg can be balanced on either end on any day of the year. Hint: you need a rock-steady surface, an egg that is free of bumps or flaws in the ends of the shell, and a steady hand. The egg must be held in place until the liquid contents settle and become stable. If you have selected the proper center of gravity, it will stand. For the cheaters out there: hard-boil the egg, and it will be much easier. The exact center of gravity varies, mostly due to natural variations in the position of the air pocket at the large end and the location of the yolk between the two ends. Many eggs balance in a position not quite true to vertical.

If there were any physical reason that the vernal equinox contributed to facility in egg standing, then the exact same physical laws would apply to the autumnal equinox (which has never been credited).

Gary Lee Phillips
Computer Services Librarian
Columbia College
Chicago, IL

Pineapple Puzzler

 We have a patron who is looking for information on the symbolism of the pineapple. She has heard it as a symbol of hospitality. We have tried the *Folklore Encyclopedia* and a book on symbols, but no luck.

Skip Booth
Anne Arundel County Public Library
Crofton Branch
Annapolis, MD

 This is from the *Dictionary of Ornament* by Philippa Lewis and Gillian Darley:

Pineapple—ancient symbol of fertility, particularly in the Middle East, and, from the late 17th Century, a symbol of hospitality in Europe and, subsequently, America, hence its use on gate piers, guest beds and bedrooms, at points of entrance and as a center-piece in tableware.

Joy Tillotson
Information Services Librarian
Queen Elizabeth II Library
Memorial University of Newfoundland
St. John's, Newfoundland
Canada

 I had this question some time ago. Here are my sources:

1. From the Colonial Williamsburg Foundation, in a book by Tina C. Jeffrey and Claude Jones, Jr., Consultant, entitled *Williamsburg Christmas Decorations*: "The Pineapple, a favorite fruit used in Xmas decorations in Williamsburg, was the traditional symbol of hospitality in the eighteenth century. Historians are uncertain why—perhaps because it was scarce and expensive—the pineapple may have come to mean extravagant hospitality to our ancestors."

2. From the Preservation Society of Newport County: "The Preservation Society's logo was inspired by the carved pineapple crowning the classic pedimented doorway of the Hunter House, which was the first acquisition and restoration project. The Pineapple became known as the symbol of hospitality in colonial times when sea captains would return home with the exotic fruit from trading expeditions in the southern seas. It would be placed on a post in front of the captain's home to signify his safe return

and that all his friends were invited to stop in and share the good
fortune of his successful voyage."

Jerry Rafats
Reference Librarian
National Agricultural Library
Beltsville, MD

□ □ □

Recipe Rumor

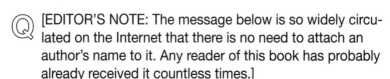

[EDITOR'S NOTE: The message below is so widely circulated on the Internet that there is no need to attach an
author's name to it. Any reader of this book has probably
already received it countless times.]

Okay, everyone . . . a true story of justice in the good old
U.S. of A. Thought y'all might enjoy this; if nothing else, it
shows Internet justice, if it can be called that.

My daughter and I had just finished a salad at Neiman-
Marcus Cafe in Dallas and decided to have a small
dessert. Because our family are such cookie lovers, we
decided to try the "Neiman-Marcus Cookie." It was so
excellent that I asked if they would give me the recipe, and
they said with a small frown, "I'm afraid not." "Well," I said,
"would you let me buy the recipe?" With a cute smile, the
waitress said, "Yes." I asked how much and she replied,
"two fifty." I said with approval, "Just add it to my tab."

Thirty days later, I received my Visa statement from
Neiman-Marcus and it was $285.00. I looked again and I
remembered I had spent only $9.95 for two salads and
about $20 for a scarf. As I glanced at the bottom of the
statement, it said, "Cookie Recipe—$250.00." Boy, was I
upset!! I called Neiman's Accounting Dept. and told them
the waitress said it was "two fifty," and I didn't realize she
meant $250 for a cookie recipe.

I asked them to take back the recipe and reduce my bill
and they said they were sorry, but because all the recipes

were this expensive so that not just anyone would dupli-cate any of their bakery recipes, the bill would stand.

I waited, thinking of how I could get even or try to get any of my money back.

I just said, "Okay, you folks got my $250 and now I'm going to have $250 worth of fun." I told her that I was going to see to it that every cookie lover would have a $250 cookie recipe from Neiman-Marcus for nothing. She replied, "I wish you wouldn't do this." I said, "I'm sorry but this is the only way I feel I could get even," and I will.

So, here it is, and please pass it to someone else or run a few copies. I paid for it; now you can have it for free.

(Recipe may be halved.)

2 cups butter

4 cups flour

2 tsp. baking soda

2 cups white sugar

5 cups blended oatmeal★★

24 oz. chocolate chips

2 cups brown sugar

1 tsp. salt

1 8 oz. Hershey Bar (grated)

4 eggs

2 tsp. baking powder

3 cups chopped nuts (your choice)

2 tsp. vanilla

Cream butter and both sugars.

Add eggs and vanilla.

Mix together flour, oatmeal, salt, baking powder, and baking soda.

Add chocolate chips, Hershey Bar, and nuts.

Roll into balls and place two inches apart on a cookie sheet.

Bake for 10 minutes at 375 degrees.

Makes 112 cookies.

*Measure oatmeal and blend in blender to a fine powder.

The overpriced-recipe story type predates the Internet by a few decades.

A great source for this is Jan Harold Brunvand's *Curses! Broiled Again! The Hottest Urban Legends Going.*

I recommend all of Professor Brunvand's urban legend books, especially *The Baby Train & Other Lusty Urban Legends,* which includes a type-index to the urban legends in the other books.

For the record, for the Archives, and for anyone to forward to anyone else who's circulating the blended-oatmeal chocolate chip recipe, here is a summary of Brunvand's history, culled from *Curses!* (pp. 219–226). Brunvand's history is a highly readable narrative. My summary is a cold time line:

1940s: A chocolate cake recipe includes a story of paying $25 to "a restaurant down south somewhere."

1948: *Massachusetts Cooking Rules, Old and New* includes a recipe for "$25 Fudge Cake," with a story about someone having to pay $25 to a railroad chef for the recipe.

1949: A story circulates in Milwaukee about someone having to pay $100 instead of $1 for "Mrs. Stevens Fudge Recipe."

1950s: Rumors circulate, accompanied by a variety of recipes, about a "Red Velvet Cake" someone "bought" from New York's Waldorf-Astoria Hotel for $1,000.

1982: The Mrs. Fields company moves to Utah. A rumor is circulating about an overpriced cookie recipe from a restaurant.

1983: The rumor acquires the Mrs. Fields connection.

1987: The 450 outlets of Mrs. Fields Cookies display a poster debunking rumors that someone bought their recipe for $250. (Fliers had been circulating previously, retelling the story of $2.50/$250, pretty much as we've just seen it, but with the source being Mrs. Fields's.)

1987: In St. Louis, a recipe circulates as the $350 Union Station cookie recipe.

Chicago, undated: There is a mint fudge recipe circulated with a story about Marshall Field's.

1988: The Mrs. Fields story appears in the American Embassy newsletter (*Tales of Vienna*) in Vienna, cited as coming from diplomats in Budapest.

1988: The Neiman-Marcus version of the cookie story is documented, though it probably circulated earlier. Neiman-Marcus goes on record at this point, saying that the story is untrue and that "the store does not even serve or sell cookies." This documentation is by columnist Martha Hertz of the *Athens* [Georgia] *Banner-Herald,* January 25, 1988, and February 29, 1988. The Neiman-Marcus cookie story gets the widest circulation of any of the similar legends. ·

Brunvand's earlier book, *The Vanishing Hitchhiker,* includes more on the "Red Velvet Cake." Meanwhile, Brunvand's student researchers say that the blended-oatmeal recipe is too dry to be a Mrs. Fields cookie.

Nina Gilbert
Department of Music, School of the Arts
University of California, Irvine
Irvine, CA

4 Colors

Once in a Blue Moon

Q Next month, September, will be a "blue moon" month, i.e., a month in which there are two full moons. A local reporter has asked why it is referred to as "blue." We have searched high and low but can find no reference to why the color is blue except for a reference called *The International Encyclopedia of Astronomy* by Moore, which mentions an occasional change in atmospheric conditions that causes the moon to appear blue. *But* this entry makes no reference to the two full moons within the same month.

Marcia Frasier
Principal Librarian
Santa Maria Public Library
Santa Maria, CA

A According to Block and Bird's three-minute public radio program, *Earth and Sky,* the present blue moon occurs in August in North America but in September in Europe because of the position of the moon in relation to Greenwich Mean Time. They also tackled, briefly, the change in meaning of *blue moon* from "once in a very long time" to the second moon to occur in a calendar month. Unfortunately, I was in the car when I heard the program, so I do not have all the details. They indicated that the first reference in print their researchers could find to the second definition was a 1946 article by J. Hugh Pruett in *Sky and Telescope.* I missed the name of the person they were quoting, but they said he attributed the origin of the term *blue moon* to a desire to keep the order of the named moons (harvest moon, hunter's moon) straight.

John Henderson
Reference Librarian
Ithaca College
Ithaca, NY

We have a citation in our fugitive file for *Astronomy,* July 1985, p. 47.

A longer article, "It's a Once in a Blue Moon Event," appeared in the *Los Angeles Times* of May 31, 1988.

In addition to a blue moon being the second full moon in the same month (also called a quintain month, according to a reference center newsletter of 1991 that we receive), the moon can also be truly blue or green due to atmospheric conditions, when there is a lot of smoke in the atmosphere from a major forest fire or volcanic eruption, for instance. The *Los Angeles Times* article states that the origin of the term *blue moon* has not been documented, but according to Leroy Doggett, an astronomer with the U.S. Naval Observatory, it may relate to ancient or medieval sightings of blue-colored moons. The director of Griffith Observatory (Los Angeles), Edwin Krupp, is quoted as saying, "It wasn't until sometime during the 19th Century that the term 'once in a blue moon' . . . was linked to astronomy . . . "

Judy Swink
Reference Librarian
Serra Cooperative Library System
San Diego, CA

Whence Pink and Blue?

 How did the colors pink and blue become associated with girls and boys?

 Here's what readers of "The Exchange" (*RQ,* Fall 1987, p. 22) had to say in response to this question (summarized):

An ancient belief held that evil spirits hovered over the nursery. These spirits were supposedly allergic to some colors, most particularly blue, because of its association with the sky. Boys then were protected with blue clothes, but girls, being much less important, weren't given any distinctive color. . . . The pink color came later in European legends claiming girls were born inside a pink rose. This latter-day legend also suggested that boys were to be found in blue cabbage patches.

Sources cited for this info were Brasch, *How Did It Begin* (pp. 22–23) and Feldman, *Imponderables: The Solution to the Mysteries of Everyday Life* (p. 29).

Charles Anderson
Editor, "The Exchange," RQ
(Reference and User Services Quarterly,
a publication of the American Library Association)
Bellevue, WA

 From *Gender Shock* by Phyllis Burke, p. 141:

Originally, pink was a boy's color and blue was for girls. Before World War II, blue signified "delicate and dainty," and pink represented "a stronger, more decided color." It would be virtually impossible in 1995 to find an article of boy's clothing in pink, because it would be considered "unnatural." Colors have extraordinary power, but the meaning of those colors is subject to change, as are styles and cuts of clothing.

Burke footnotes this paragraph as follows on p. 265:

—Marjorie Garber, *Vested Interests: Cross-Dressing and Cultural Anxiety,* p. 1.

Also, Garber (pp. 25–32) gives strict dress codes, or sumptuary laws, of Renaissance times that severely regulated what one could wear based on social class, etc.

Jamie McGrath
Senior Librarian
Alameda Free Library Reference Department
Alameda, CA

□ □ □

Because They're Cowardly?

 Q I have a patron who needs to know why pencils (most of them) are yellow. We've read some excellent articles on the history of the pencil, but alas, the answer wasn't there.

Lindsay Van Sicklen
Librarian
Commonwealth College
Richmond, VA

 A Henry Petroski, in his authoritative *The Pencil,* offers several explanations, some of them interrelated (pp. 161–163).

1. Koh-I-Noor pencils, a leading quality brand introduced in the 1890s, might have been yellow and black (the "lead" is black) to honor the Austrian colors.

2. Yellow suggested an "Oriental" provenance for the graphite, when the best graphite was Asian.

3. The great success of the premium Koh-I-Noor brand made yellow a standard. A possibly apocryphal experiment among twentieth-century office workers, who were given a supply of otherwise identical green and yellow pencils, established a strong bias in favor of yellow.

4. Yellow is simply visible, making it easier to retrieve a misplaced pencil.

(Before and since the 1890s, pencils were made in a variety of colors, with clear finish sometimes regarded as a mark of quality as early as the 1860s.)

Joe Barnes
Library Director
Shepherd College
Shepherdstown, WV

5 Symbols

Mystical Money

Q This should have been easy, but for some reason I can't find a printed citation. A patron wants to know the meaning of the pyramid with an eye on the dollar bill.

Patricia Lyons Basu
Library Director
Hiram College
Hiram, OH

A The explanation that the eye on the back of the dollar is part of an Illuminati plot is one that is advanced by Pat Robertson in his book *The New World Order.* He also claims that the Illuminati instigated the French Revolution, inspired Marx and Engels to write the *Communist Manifesto,* penetrated the international financial community through the Rothschilds, and were involved in the assassination of Lincoln.

—Source: *Washington Post,* October 11, 1992.

A more traditional explanation than the Illuminati is that the symbols come from freemasonry. The pyramid represents the Masonic notion that freemasonry began in ancient times. The eye is the all-seeing eye of the Supreme Architect of the Universe. The symbols are taken from the Great Seal of the United States. The Great Seal was officially adopted in 1782. It was designed by a committee headed by Benjamin Franklin, Thomas Jefferson, and John Adams. It first appeared on our money in 1935.

—Sources: *Atlanta Journal and Constitution,* May 3, 1993; *Houston Chronicle,* January 26, 1993.

Andrew H. Steinberg
Law Librarianship Student
University of Washington
Seattle, WA

 The following is from Alvin J. Schmidt, *Fraternal Organizations,* p. 122:

The seal's reverse side with its All-Seeing Eye set in a triangle, surrounded by a golden glory, is so obviously Masonic that anyone with only a rudimentary acquaintance with speculative Masonry recognizes the Masonic symbolism here. The unfinished pyramid below the All-Seeing Eye reminds a Mason of the soul's immortality, which he will complete in eternity. It also recalls the unfinished temple of Solomon (a familiar story to every informed Mason) that resulted because the master architect was killed.

Donald Barclay
New Mexico State University Library
Las Cruces, NM

 My colleague here, Barbara Friedman, found information in the *Facts on File Dictionary of Symbolism* under the entry for "eye":

In Christian iconography, the eye, surrounded by sunbeams or inside a triangle with its apex pointed upward, is a well-known symbol of divine omnipresence.

Sudie Blanchard
Information Librarian
Greenwich Library
Greenwich, CT

 From *Facts About United States Money* (Dept. of the Treasury, 1976, sudocs T 1.40/976):

The selection of designs used on our paper currency . . . is a responsibility of the Secretary of the Treasury . . . None of the letters, numbers, or symbols on currency . . . has any sectarian significance.

The new seal of the Dept. of the Treasury, approved on Jan. 29, 1968, is overprinted on the face of each note . . . the new seal bears the date "1789," the year of the Dept.'s creation. Balance scales, representing justice; a key; the emblem of official authority; and a chevron with 13 stars for the original states . . .

Both the obverse and the reverse of the Great Seal of the United States, adopted in 1782, are reproduced on the back of $1 bills. The obverse depicts an American eagle breasted by our national shield. The eagle holds in its right talon an olive branch of 13 leaves and 13 berries symbolic of peace. In the left talon are 13 arrows signifying the original colonies' fight for liberty. A ribbon flying from the beak of the eagle is inscribed with the Latin motto, *e pluribus unum,* translated "one out of many," in reference to the unity of the 13 colonies as one government. Over the eagle's head is a constellation of 13 five-pointed stars surrounded by a wreath of clouds.

The reverse of the seal depicts a pyramid, with 1776, the year of the Declaration of Independence, in the roman numerals MDCCLXXVI on its base. The pyramid represents permanence and strength. Its unfinished condition symbolizes that there was still work to be done to form a more perfect . . . Union. The eye in the triangular glory represents an all-seeing Deity. The words *annuit coeptis,* translated as "he [God] has favored our undertakings," refer to the many interpositions of Divine Providence in the forming of our government; *novus ordo seclorum,* translated as "a new order of the ages," signifies a new American era.

Wess Wessling
Reference Librarian
State Library of North Carolina
Raleigh, NC

The Other Adjective

 Q What is the feminine equivalent of the word *phallic*?

A My wife and I use the term *yonic,* from *yoni,* the stylized representation of the female genitalia symbolizing the feminine principle in Hindu cosmology.

—Source: *Merriam Webster's Collegiate Dictionary* (1994).

Bill Thomas
Reference Librarian
County of Los Angeles Public Library
Lancaster, CA

Heart Hunt

 Q How did the heart become a symbol for love in popular culture?

A The *Dictionary of Symbolism* by Hans Biedermann has the following as part of its entry on *heart:*

From the Middle Ages onward love poetry romanticizes the heart, . . . and in art it is soon stylized with anatomically incorrect bosom-like upper edges and associated at times with earthly, at times with mystical and heavenly, love.

Martha Sink
Librarian
Central North Carolina Regional Library
Burlington, NC

 A Carl G. Liungman in *Dictionary of Symbols* (1991) discusses the heart symbol and some of its meanings in different times and cultures (all in two pages), from Ice Age Europeans (meaning unknown) to Greeks living before the common era (symbol of Eros and Dionysus) to modern

Swedes (strongly associated with the buttocks and defecation, as it is the sign used to denote a toilet for both sexes). It is difficult to transcribe Liungman's text, since much of it includes the actual signs and symbols.

John Henderson
Reference Librarian
Ithaca College Library
Ithaca, NY

More Heart Hunt

 How did the cartoonish heart symbol seen on greeting cards and bumper stickers originate? It is not shaped like the actual human heart.

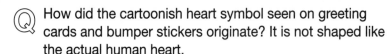 Peter J. Dorman, *The Book of Hearts,* p. 12, describes a paleolithic cave painting:

Drawn more or less like the now traditional, symmetrical form, the hearts of the elephant and the bison, for example, are clearly depicted and accurately placed within the outline drawing of the entire animal.

In other words, it certainly *does* resemble the anatomical heart, stripped of detail.

Carolyn Caywood
Bayside Area Librarian
Virginia Beach, VA

#?

 What is the correct name for the symbol #?

 Octothorp is listed in *Merriam-Webster's Collegiate Dictionary* with the definition "the symbol #." The etymology is given as "octo- + thorp, of unknown origin; fr. the eight points on its circumference." Other terms for # include *cross-hatch, pound sign,* and *number sign.*

Fred R. Shapiro
Associate Librarian for Public Services
Yale Law School
New Haven, CT

 The following is from the alt.usage.english FAQ by Mark Israel, which has the answers to many questions that come up on Stumpers:

"#" has three principal names relating to uses for it:

"number (sign)," as in "the team finished in the #5 position";

"pound (sign)," referring to weight, as in "a 5# bag of potatoes";

"sharp (sign)," in music, as in "the key of C# major."

Of these, "pound" is the most widely used in the U.S., but confuses people who expect that term to mean the symbol for sterling currency (which was located on British typewriter keyboards in the same place as "#" is found on U.S. keyboards). "Number sign," adopted by ANSI/CCITT, is unambiguous, but little known in both the U.K. and the U.S.; and "sharp" is not widely used. Computer users in the U.K. usually call the symbol a "hash," from its appearance.

Elizabeth B. Thomsen
Member Services Manager
NOBLE: North of Boston Library Exchange
Danvers, MA

□ □ □

@?

 Does the "at" symbol (@) have a special name?

 In response to your query, the *Illustrated Computer Dictionary for Dummies* by Dan Gookin et al. indicates that the

"@" or "at" symbol goes by many names, including *at sign, about, strudel, rose,* or *cabbage.*

Jason Biggers
Webmaster
Tampa-Hillsborough County Public Library System
Tampa, FL

 According to the excellent alt.usage.english FAQ by Mark Israel, "The longest name for '@' is 'commercial at sign'; the first and last words may be omitted. The official ANSI/CCITT name is 'commercial at.' "

Fred R. Shapiro
Associate Librarian for Public Services
Yale Law Library
New Haven, CT

 The commonest reference I have found for @ is "the at sign." Many college and unabridged dictionaries have labeled it "commercial at sign" or something similar to identify its application to the pricing or quantification of produce or the like. Of course, its current application in e-mail has created fresh interest in its origin. Another new application of @ is in chemistry, where it is used to identify molecules captured inside other molecules without chemical bonding (i.e., in fullerenes). The origin is probably from a stylistic version of Latin *ad* meaning "at." According to the *Oxford English Dictionary,* it first appeared in English writing in the early fourteenth century. For more information see *The Barnhart Dictionary Companion* (vols. 8.1 and 8.4).

David K. Barnhart
Editor
Barnhart Dictionary Companion
Cold Spring, NY

 Summary of "The Man Who Put the @ in e-mail" by Sasha Cavender, *San Francisco Chronicle,* October 23, 1996, p. B3:

When Ray Tomlinson, a computer engineer who loved to experiment, put the @ sign in the first e-mail message in 1971, he had no idea he would change how the world communicates. . . .

Tomlinson, 55, wasn't seeking anything grandiose when he arrived in 1967 at BBN, a computer consulting firm here [Cambridge, MA] that built the ARPANET, the predecessor to the Internet . . .

He was just experimenting, looking for some sort of standardized coding to send mail from one machine at BBN to another. "In the jargon of the times, it was a hack," he said.

His solution was a program called SNDMSG and the now ubiquitous address format that lets messages travel easily, even between incompatible machines. . . .

The @ symbol separates the person from the place, so as not to confuse computers routing the mail.

Tomlinson considered several symbols before choosing the @. He needed a character that would never be part of the user's name. That left the punctuation symbols, but which ones?

. . . the @ sign is clear and makes sense: so-and-so at a certain location.

Tomlinson sent the first e-mail message with @ to himself at another machine at BBN. "It worked!" he said. "I logged into one machine, sent it to another, and there it was."

"I wrote the first program to send e-mail via network and I chose the @ sign. The first is what's important, the second is what everyone remembers. . . ."

The article also includes the names of the @ symbol in various languages and some cute graphics, e.g., France—

petit escargot (little snail); Norway—*kanel-bolle* (a spiral-shaped cinnamon cake).

Kathy Greenstein
Cataloger
Alameda County Library
Fremont, CA

$?

 Why do we use an *s* with two lines through it to indicate "dollar"?

Jan Pike
Library Assistant
Mesquite Branch Library
Phoenix, AZ

 According to the pamphlet *Facts About United States Money,* by the Department of the Treasury:

The origin of the $ sign has been variously accounted for, with perhaps the most widely accepted explanation being that it is the evolution of the Mexican or Spanish "P's" for pesos, or piastres, or pieces of eight. The theory, derived from a study of old manuscripts, is that the "S" gradually came to be written over the "P," developing a close equivalent of the $ mark. It was widely used before the adoption of the United States dollar in 1785.

Su Vathanaprida
Reference Librarian
King County Library System
Seattle, WA

6 Language

Is That a Real Name?

 Someone recently asked if there is a list of names that might have a double meaning, names like Sandy Beech, Dusty Rhodes, Crystal Clear, Beau Tique, May Flowers, etc. Does anyone know of such a list?

If you do not know of a list, but have your favorites, please send those to me as well.

V. Lonnie Lawson
Reference Librarian
Ward Edwards Library
Central Missouri State University
Warrensburg, MO

 There is (or at least was three or four years ago) a lawyer in Wilmington, Delaware, named Perry Goldlust . . . I kid you not.

John Lupton
LAN Specialist
SAS Communications & Networking
University of Pennsylvania
Philadelphia, PA

Don't forget:

Chevy Chase

Slim Pickens

and, um, Pussy Galore

Do fictional names count? If so, check out any Thomas Pynchon novel, e.g., Joaquin Stick, "Mucho" Mass, and so forth. Not to mention prank phone calls of the Bart

Simpson variety ("Amanda Hugginkiss . . . I'm looking for Amanda Hugginkiss . . . ?").

Jonathan Foote
Providence, RI

 A recent issue of the *Journal of the American Medical Association* had a humorous article about doctors' names, listing names like Dr. Nurse, Dr. Cure, and Dr. Doctor. I happened to see this when I was visiting friends last winter, one of whom is a doctor (Dr. Markowitz, not Dr. Doctor).

I found the citation just now on Medline. It was indexed, appropriately enough, under major terms NAMES and PHYSICIANS and minor terms HUMAN and WIT AND HUMOR. I also found two letters and a response to the original article. The letter from Dr. Hug said that he worked for a while with Dr. Kiss. The other letter noted coauthors Smith and Wesson who, the writer surmises, shot from the hip.

Here are the citations:

A piece of my mind. Calling Dr Doctor.
Bennett, H. J.
JAMA. 1992 Dec 2. P 3060.
Dr Doctor calls back [letter]
Balestra, D. J.
JAMA. 1993 Apr 7. P 1637.
Dr Doctor calls back [letter]
Hug, H. R.
JAMA. 1993 Apr 7. P 1637.

From time to time one sees articles in the popular press about names that match their owners' occupations. I think Dear Abby has been running some in the last several months, for instance. I'm sure we all have anecdotes. For instance, a federal appeals judge is named Judge Wisdom (but if you add his middle name, it's Judge John Minor Wisdom). A professor here at the University of Washington is named Professor Dull—fortunately, I understand he does not live up to his name.

Mary Whisner
Head of Reference
Gallagher Law Library
University of Washington
Seattle, WA

 To everyone interested in the names with double meanings, let me recommend three books compiled and annotated by John Train:

Remarkable Names of Real People, or How to Name Your Baby. (Don't be fooled by the subtitle, most of them are pretty bizarre.)

Even More Remarkable Names.

John Train's Most Remarkable Names. (I haven't seen this one, but its cataloging record says it is a compendium of names from the first two books, plus some new ones.)

Not all of the names listed have double meanings, but all are very strange, and Train swears they are all real people. My favorite from *Even More* is Ophelia Bumps of Richmond, Virginia. Fair Hooker and Pearl Harbor are also listed.

Others from *Even More* include Ecstasy Goon of the Wisconsin Historical Society and J. Fido Spot of West Palm Beach, Florida. And how about Lovey Nookey Good of the Texas State Health Department?

One name not in the books is that of a young woman who worked for me in Key West many years ago, Stormy Haven.

Elizabeth Henderson
Reference Librarian
Lynchburg College
Lynchburg, VA

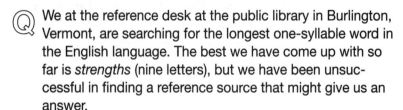

I Stretched My Strengths

Q We at the reference desk at the public library in Burlington, Vermont, are searching for the longest one-syllable word in the English language. The best we have come up with so far is *strengths* (nine letters), but we have been unsuccessful in finding a reference source that might give us an answer.

Robert J. Resnik
Reference Librarian
Fletcher Free Library
Burlington, VT

 A Have you considered the (admittedly unauthoritative) word *schmaltzed*? As in: The play wasn't doing well at the box office, so the writers schmaltzed it up a little.

My dictionary lists schmaltz only as a noun, but I'm sure I've heard it used as a verb on occasion.

If *strengths* is, in fact, one of the longest monosyllables in English, it is by no means the only one with nine letters. Walt Howe gave the example *straights,* but the list can be *stretched* out indefinitely; we've only just *scratched* the surface. . . .

I can cite some authorities that give *strengths* as the longest English word with only one vowel:

Dickson's Word Treasury by Paul Dickson, p. 208 has this entry:

STRENGTHS. The Reverend Solomon Ream claims in his *Curiosities of the English Language* that this is probably the longest word in English with only one vowel—to say nothing of its being one of the longest one-syllable words in the language. . . .

I briefly looked through Ream's book, but there didn't seem to be any additional information relevant to our subject.

More conclusively, according to "Steeds Ambidextrously Spoonfeed Desserts: Records from the World of Words," an article by Eric Albert in *Games* magazine, June 1992, p. 8, *strengths* holds the record for "longest word with a single vowel."

At the end of that article the author credits *Word Ways* magazine as the source for many of the examples. I don't have access to *Word Ways,* but you might consider checking it for further information.

Russell Perkins
Winston-Salem, NC

 Russell Perkins and others have pointed out various nine-letter, one-syllable words such as *stretched* and *scratched.* However, the rec.puzzles Archives provides a ten-letter one: *scraunched.* An eleven-letter word is given in brackets: *squirrelled.* Presumably the brackets are meant to indicate that the monosyllabicity of this word is questionable.

The rec.puzzles Archives also gives *scratchbrushed* as the answer for the longest two-syllable word in English.

Fred R. Shapiro
Associate Librarian for Public Services
Yale Law School
New Haven, CT

Double Double Toil and Trouble

 I have a patron who says there is a word in the English language with four sets of double letters in it, not necessarily in order.

We have exhausted our resources looking for such a word.
Does anyone know what it is?

Rex Miller
Director
Petoskey Public Library
Petoskey, MI

 In a long-ago "Fact and Fancy" column by L. M. Boyd, there was *raccoonnookkeeper* which is actually six sets of double letters—I never checked the dictionary to see if same was listed, though. *Raccoonnook* would certainly be four if they didn't need a keeper!

L. Jeanne Powers
Reference Librarian
Bristol Public Library
Bristol, VA/TN

 This question is answered in the archives of the news-group rec.puzzles:

most consecutive doubled letters	bookkeeper, bookkeeping
most doubled letters	possessionlessness, possessionlessnesses
	successlessness, successlessnesses

As far as the *raccoonnookkeeper* is concerned, I had heard that someone held that position at the San Diego Zoo. I always assumed this was apocryphal, but the organization that publishes *Zoonooz* obviously has some interest in wordplay.

Fred W. Helenius
Boulder, CO

 I don't know if place-names count, but there is a suburb of Sydney named *Woolloomooloo,* five doublings even if you do not count the *w* as a double "u"!

Katherine Cummings
Reference Librarian
Macquarie University
Sydney, New South Wales
Australia

□ □ □

Weird Leisure

 The following quote is a mnemonic for remembering words with the spelling "ei" rather than "ie." We are trying to determine whether the quote is complete, i.e., does it contain all the "ei" words?

Neither of the foreign sovereigns seized the weird heights at their leisure.

Victoria Kline, Ph.D.
Librarian
Pasadena, CA

 It's a weighty question, neighbor, but either I'm a bad speller or you're missing some "ei" words. Probably need to rein in our enthusiasm before receiving our crowns and beginning our reign as spelling champs.

Here's the mnemonic I learned in elementary school:

I before E,

except after C,

and when sounding "A"

as in Neighbor and Weigh.

Mary Whisner
Head of Reference
Gallagher Law Library
University of Washington
Seattle, WA

 I don't think the quote is intended to include all the "ei" words, just ones that do not fit the coda to the original "I before E" rule, which is "when sounding 'A,' as in Neighbor and Weigh."

Elizabeth B. Thomsen
Member Services Manager
NOBLE: North of Boston Library Exchange
Danvers, MA

Even if used only as an adjunct to the standard "except after C and when sounding 'A' " rule, the coda is still "sleight"-ly deficient.

Michael Reagan
Circulation Unit Coordinator
Oviatt Library
California State University
Northridge, CA

7 Words and Phrases

Politically Correct in 1793

 When did the phrase *politically correct* surface? Who coined it, and in what context? I see in *Webster's Ninth New Collegiate Dictionary* that *affirmative action* has been around since 1965.

I'm my own patron here, as it were (I mean, I'm not a librarian . . .). I'm writing a column for the *Choral Journal* addressing the issue of political correctness in choral texts (such as generic love poems that idealize a woman for being slender, white, and frail and having tiny feet; or songs that glorify situations that would today be recognized as date rape).

Nina Gilbert
Department of Music, School of the Arts
University of California, Irvine
Irvine, CA

Amazingly, the phrase *politically correct* goes back as far as 1793. In that year it appeared in the landmark U.S. Supreme Court decision, *Chisholm v. Georgia.* In this case Justice James Wilson wrote in his opinion: "The states, rather than the People, for whose sakes the States exist, are frequently the objects which attract and arrest our principal attention. . . . Sentiments and expressions of this inaccurate kind prevail in our common, even in our convivial, language. Is a toast asked? 'The United States,' instead of the 'People of the United States,' is the toast given. This is not politically correct."

The usage here, referring to linguistic etiquette, is actually quite close to the modern meaning, although without the satire now associated with the expression.

The phrase is found occasionally thereafter—Vladimir Nabokov and Czeslaw Milosz both used it—but it began its real life in the late 1960s as a positive term in radical literature. Used consistently throughout the 1970s and '80s, the term got hijacked by conservatives around 1990.

Fred R. Shapiro
Associate Librarian for Public Services
Yale Law School
New Haven, CT

□ □ □

"Flushed with Pride"

Q I heard on a CBC Toronto radio broadcast a few years ago an answer to a question I had been using to challenge students not to believe everything they read in books, even reference books in our library. The *People's Almanac,* p. 911, tells the story of the inventor of the brassiere, Otto Titzling. I was sure this was untrue, and found ways to prove it wrong. But I never was able to discover the source of this fictional person. In the radio broadcast, someone provided the answer. A person invented several fictional biographies of inventors and presented them as factual. In addition to Otto Titzling, Thomas Crapper was invented as the inventor of the flush toilet. I have occasionally tackled this question myself, but I have not been able to discover any other source to confirm the radio broadcast. So, does anyone out there know the author of fake biographies and creator of Otto Titzling and Thomas Crapper?

John Henderson
Reference Librarian
Ithaca College Library
Ithaca, NY

A Wallace Reyburn wrote the book *Flushed with Pride: The Story of Thomas Crapper,* and also a 1971 item called *Bust-*

Up: The Uplifting Tale of Otto Titzling and the Development of the Bra. This one seemed to be obvious to even the most gullible of catalogers, and hence generally gets the subject subheading "—Humor" whereas the Thomas Crapper volume seems to be usually cataloged as straight history. Most of Reyburn's other books are novels, or nonfiction on rugby or on British television; if he did any other "invented inventor" biographies at book length, they are not obvious.

A bio of Reyburn appears in volume 1 (new revised series) of *Contemporary Authors,* if anyone is interested. He has worked as a journalist and freelancer in New Zealand, England, and Canada, for such magazines as *New Liberty, Queen,* and the *Toronto Telegram,* mostly as a features editor. So who knows how many hoax "features" may be found buried in back numbers of those publications. . . .

Dennis Lien
Reference Librarian
Wilson Library
University of Minnesota
Minneapolis, MN

 Just a small point of reference turns up in *Panati's Extraordinary Origins of Everyday Things.* According to this, there have been versions of flush toilets in use as far back as the ancient Egyptians. In later times, a version was installed for Queen Elizabeth I, designed by her godson Sir John Harrington. Unfortunately, Harrington wrote a book about it, titled *The Metamorphosis of Ajax* (Ajax being a pun on the word "Jake," then slang for chamber pot). And QEI got angry and banished him.

Another version appeared in 1775, patented by a British mathematician and watchmaker, Alexander Cumming (again, per Panati). This one featured a design to entrap water, thus separating the user from decomposing material and the accompanying odor.

There is no mention of Thomas Crapper.*

The brassiere, according to Panati, has been around in one form or another since ancient Roman times. Various designs came and went, but the first modern brassiere was designed by Mary Phelps Jacobs, who helped kill the corset. Her attempts to market her brassiere design apparently failed, but she eventually sold her patent to Warner Brothers Corset Co. of Bridgeport, Connecticut for $1,500. At the time of Panati's book (1987), the patent was valued at about $15 million.

Again, there is no mention of anyone named Otto Titzling.*

The work I have referenced is *Panati's Extraordinary Origins of Everyday Things* by Charles Panati. For those who are interested, Mr. Panati has also published *Panati's Extraordinary Endings of Practically Everything and Everybody.*

Katie Buller
Madison, WI

 A few salient points:

1. Thomas Crapper was real and did own a firm that manufactured flushable toilets, among other gear.

2. He did not invent the flush toilet. There were flushable water-closets by the end of the seventeenth century.

3. The juxtaposition of the nouns *crap* and *Crapper* is coincidental, to the extent that the surname Crapper (a Lancashire family) is a

---

There is a small reference to these "people" at the back of the book, debunking both legends. The book Flushed with Pride *supposedly reads like a genuine biography for a while; then the double entendres and puns begin to reveal it as a hoax (i.e., "high water mark in his career," ". . . after many dry runs," etc.). The same treatment was apparently used on the Titzling book. To author Reyburn's credit, he used many genuine references in his foot-notes, and eventually enough people took his works to be "researched" well enough to be used as references in other writings. Naturally, most of these writers apparently did not bother to actually read them. Times haven't changed much, have they?*

variant of Cropper, from the Middle English *crop(en)* "to pick or pluck," from *crop* "produce"; from Old English *cropp* "swelling, head of a plant"; while *crap* "excrement" comes from the same late Old English or early Middle English *crop* "produce," according to the *Oxford English Dictionary.*

4. Thomas Crapper's name would not be of any interest at all, but for the twentieth-century mania for the titillatingly scatological. (After all, it hardly excited much notice in the last century, did it? Nor was he embarrassed by it, apparently.)

Frank Young
Falls Church, VA

 As a child in the 1950s I learned that we were descended from the family that invented the flush toilet. Although the family name was now Bovey from the Devon area, it had once been Crapper-Bovey or Bovey-Crapper (I'm not sure if it was hyphenated). I have a Sunday School book given to Bertram Crapper at Whitechurch in Devon from 1895. The name Crapper is a perfectly good English name.

This should allay some fears, e.g., that the name Crapper is an invention.

Robert Moore
Senior Research Engineer
Brown University
Providence, RI

 The following is from the *Science and Technology Desk Reference,* p. 83:

But it was not until 1861 that British sanitary engineer Thomas Crapper (1837–1910) offered his major innovation—a mechanism that shut off the flow of clean water when the tank filled.

Sources:

Tom Burnam, *Dictionary of Misinformation,* p. 56.
Nell DuVall, *Domestic Technology,* pp. 363, 366.

Richard B. Manchester, *Mammoth Book of Fascinating Information,* pp. 452–456.

John Creech
Electronic Resources Librarian and Assistant Head of Reference
Central Washington University
Ellensburg, WA

 This is a summary of postings on the Thomas Crapper affair:

Thomas Crapper appears to have actually existed and was a sanitary engineer. Doubts as to his existence have been caused by the nature of a biography of him written by Wallace Reyburn in 1969 entitled *Flushed with Pride: The Story of Thomas Crapper.* The tone of the book was light-hearted, but most of it, apparently, accurate (I guess, not having seen it yet). The trouble began when two years later Reyburn wrote a second biography, but this one clearly a spoof or hoax: *Bust-Up: The Uplifting Tale of Otto Titzling and the Development of the Bra.*

If Crapper existed, certain elements of his story that are commonly presented are not true. He was not knighted, never became Sir Thomas Crapper. He was issued royal warrants for some of his work, but that recognition falls far short of being knighted. The origin of the word *crapper* to mean "toilet" as a derivation from its inventor is also questionable. Crapper was British, but the slang term *crapper* appears to have begun in the United States. The best argument that Thomas Crapper lent his name to the slang term is that it appears to have entered the language after Crapper's death. *Crap* as a slang word for feces, however, is much earlier than Crapper, his company, or his invention.

Documentary evidence of Thomas Crapper's "invention" is British patent 3964. Rosy Brewer, from the MOBAC library in Monterey, California, supplied me with a copy of the patent. The date of application is March 5th, 1891.

Date of acceptance is April 11th, 1891. Rosy also sent me several pages from an article by Ken Grabowski, called "Crap, Crapper, and Thomas Crapper: Myth or Reality (with Annotated Bibliography)," published in *Festschrift in Honor of Virgil J. Vogel,* which is a well-documented essay (even if I don't agree with all his conclusions).

John Henderson
Reference Librarian
Ithaca College Library
Ithaca, NY

□ □ □

Rule of Misinformation

The "rule of thumb" is frequently described as a dictum that "a man may beat his wife with a switch no thicker than his thumb." Does anyone know of an *authoritative* citation that relates this to a real source in legal history?

Michael A. Miranda
Benjamin F. Feinberg Library
SUNY—Plattsburgh
Plattsburgh, NY

There was a query about the supposed origin of the phrase *rule of thumb* in a supposed legal rule that a husband could beat his wife if the stick were no bigger than the thickness of a thumb. Now at last the definitive answer to this question has appeared. UCLA English Professor Henry A. Kelly has published *"Rule of Thumb* and the Folklaw of the Husband's Stick" in the September 1994 issue of *Journal of Legal Education.* In this article Kelly demonstrates that there is no basis for the etymological assertion. He also demonstrates that there is only a little evidence for the prevalence of the supposed rule itself: only "a tradition in North Carolina, supported in one case by a lower court, that a husband had a right to whip his wife with a switch smaller than his thumb" and an

English judge, Francis Buller, about 1780, who made an "unfortunate assertion that a husband could thrash his wife with impunity provided that the stick was no bigger than his thumb," an assertion that became a running joke for about a year but never became an accepted precedent.

Fred R. Shapiro
Associate Librarian for Public Services
Yale Law School
New Haven, CT

□ □ □

Giving Mosquitoes a Bad Name

 A patron remembers hearing that the word *paparazzi* derives from an Italian term for mosquito or stinging insect. However, two Italian dictionaries do not confirm this—the word is defined in one as "freelance photographer" and in the other it does not appear at all. The word for "mosquito" is entirely different, no apparent relation at all. Does anyone with a knowledge of Italian know whence the word arises? (I also tried several dictionaries of slang, American and English, and came up with zero.)

Marian Drabkin
Librarian
Richmond Public Library
Richmond, CA

There are two versions of how this name came to be. I don't find the first one convincing, but here they are.

Version I: According to the *Random House Dictionary,* 2nd edition (1995), Fellini took the name from that of a hotel-keeper in George Gissing's *By the Ionian Sea,* which Fellini was supposed to have been reading in Italian translation during the filming of *La Dolce Vita.* Fellini's own character was a photographer; therefore, . . .

Version II (in Salvatore Battaglia, *Grande Dizionario della Lingua Italiana*, 1995): Although popularized by Fellini's movie, the "name" Paparazzo was actually coined by Abruzzese screenwriter Ennio Flaiano. He took the Abruzzo dialect word *paparazzo* (clam) and applied it playfully to photographers because the opening and closing of their camera shutters reminded him of the way clams sold in his seaside hometown of Pescara opened and then snapped shut at the least provocation.

John Dyson
Department of Spanish and Portuguese
Indiana University
Bloomington, IN

□ □ □

What a Nimrod!

I'm a reference librarian at the Toronto *Globe and Mail.* Our science reporter is in the middle of a debate in the newsroom on the use of the word *nimrod(s)* to mean "big jerk(s)" or worse. It has been used a lot recently in print by our sports reporters. We have checked the sources that we have at hand, namely, Partridge's *Dictionary of Slang* and the usual dictionaries (please note that we do know that it means "mighty hunter"). After trying us, Stephen Strauss (the reporter in question) called the main public reference library here in Toronto, and they couldn't enlighten him.

We run a small article in the paper every Saturday that explains the workings of the *Globe*—how an article came about or what happened when our satellite feed went down just before deadline, etc. He feels that he might be able to turn his *nimrod* explorations into one of those articles.

Celia Donnelly
Reference Librarian
The Globe and Mail *Editorial Library*
Toronto, Ontario
Canada

If I may (with fear and trembling) offer an unprofessional speculation on this, I seem to remember Bugs Bunny calling Elmer Fudd a "nimrod" from time to time. Is it possible that this was in fact an appropriately sarcastic reference to Fudd's reputation as a "mighty hunter"? Or was *nimrod* meaning "jerk" already in common use when these cartoons came out?

Russell Perkins
Winston-Salem, NC

 Monday morning Stephen Strauss asked me to send the "Paper Making" column he wrote for Saturday's *Globe and Mail* on *nimrod* to Stumpers as a courtesy.

Serendipity is often the best friend of researchers. This was proved once again Tuesday morning when Stephen received a fax from a reader in Brampton saying, "The Bugs Bunny cartoon where he says 'What a nimrod' is *Rabbit Every Monday* with Bugs and Yosemite Sam. It was shown on Monday morning on Global TV." (Serendipity or synchronicity? Friends, both.)

A quick search of the Web on AltaVista tells us that *Rabbit Every Monday* was a Looney Tunes cartoon produced in 1951, and directed by Friz Freleng.

Rick Cash
Researcher
The Globe and Mail
Toronto, Ontario
Canada

 The alt.usage.english FAQ by Mark Israel has a section on this. It says:

Genesis 10:8–9, in describing how the Seventy Nations were founded by the descendants of Noah, says that Nimrod, son of Cush, son of Ham, son of Noah, was a "mighty man on earth" and a "mighty hunter before the LORD." The word *nimrod* is recorded

in English since 1545 with the (now obsolete) meaning "tyrant," and since 1712 with the meaning "hunter."

In contemporary U.S. slang, *nimrod* means "fool, numbskull." Rex Knepp ingeniously suggested that the origin of this was Bugs Bunny's taunt of Elmer Fudd: "So long, Nimrod." Unfortunately for this theory, Jesse Sheidlower says that Random House has two citations of *nimrod* = "numbskull" from the 1930s.

My own guess, which is only that, is that *nimrod* sounds like *numbskull* and *dimbulb*—two syllables with the M at the end of the first—and that as a result of this similarity, it has taken on this meaning. In other words, it just *sounds* like an insult, much as when Don Rickles calls someone a "hockey puck."

I do highly recommend this FAQ to anyone interested in questions of English language and usage. However, it is L-O-N-G!

Lois Aleta Fundis
Reference Librarian
Mary H. Weir Public Library
Weirton, WV

Pish Posh

 I am losing sleep over this, so please help.

I need the word that came from the "custom" when, during ship travel to Europe, one wished to have a berth on one side of the ship going and a berth on the opposite coming back.

Harriet Zook
Catalog Librarian
Sacramento, CA

 You might want to keep in mind that *posh* with the meaning of "port out, starboard home" is apparently essentially folk etymology. The *Oxford English Dictionary,* 2nd edition says: "The suggestion that this word is derived from the initials of 'port outward, starboard home' . . . is often put forward but lacks foundation. The main objections to this derivation are listed by G. Chowdharay-Best in *Mariner's Mirror* (1971) Jan. 91–2."

Bill Lowe
Reference Librarian
Westminster College
Fulton, MO

 According to the *Oxford Dictionary of English Etymology, posh* is perhaps an adjectival use of the slang noun *posh,* meaning "money" or "dandy," of unknown origin. When the *OED* or *ODEE* says something is of unknown origin, conjectural theories are usually of very little value.

Fred R. Shapiro
Associate Librarian for Public Services
Yale Law School
New Haven, CT

 Not mentioned yet is the possibility that the name of the company itself is somehow connected. At least one P&O history suggests that *posh* was a synonym for the snobbishness of P & O Steamship passengers. The P&O was formed in 1837 and began service to India in 1843 (a trip that called for berthing on the cool side). The company soon became the premier British shipping line, and is said to have invented the "cruise."

P. W. F. Brown in *Notes and Queries* (vol. 210, Nov. 1956, p. 503) preserves the Indian connection, but suggests a more plausible derivation that has no connection with shipping or the P&O. Although lacking in the 1903 Yule & Burnell *Anglo-Indian Glossary, posh* turns up in the 1916 *Hindoostani Student's Dictionary* as a Hindustani word meaning "raiment"—together with *poshak* (fine raiment) and *poshida* (clothed). *Posh* also means "clothes" in Persian, and the word became popular in India through the folk tales of Mahmoud of Ghazni and Khorasan (tenth–eleventh centuries). He went by the name of Siyah Posh because he walked the streets at night disguised in black clothes. According to Brown, "there can be little doubt that the black clothes worn by Europeans in the evening or on public or ceremonial occasions were also called Siyah Posh, and thus the meaning of 'well dressed' arose." The Persian *Siyah Posh* also means "a public occasion," adding a useful double entendre to its folk etymology.

Writing in *Notes and Queries* later (vol. 206, Oct. 1961, p. 398), the same author elaborates that the people of Kafiristan are divided into two tribes: the Siah Posh ("black robes") and Safed Posh ("white robes"). He concludes that this Urdu word entered the English language as meaning "fine clothes," probably "not earlier than 1860." He further concludes that the "port out, starboard home" myth merely points to the term's Anglo-Indian flavor. This was in answer to a January 1961 query (p. 31) that claims to have found an 1892 usage of *posh,* which predates by five years the earliest finding of the *OED* and Partridge's *Dictionary of Slang.*

T. F. Mills
Serials Librarian
University of Denver Library
Denver, CO

□ □ □

Cut to the Chase

Q A patron would like to know the meaning of the word *chase* in the expression *cut to the chase.* I checked the archives and found one example of this expression in an answer to an unrelated question. In the answer the respondent used the most common definition of the term *chase:* to pursue in order to catch or overtake. The patron is not sure that this is accurate.

John Stierman
Reference Librarian
Western Illinois University
Macomb, IL

 I was surprised to find that *cut to the chase* is generally omitted from dictionaries of words, phrases, proverbs, or quotations. I would have thought it was an old proverbial phrase with some arcane origin. I then searched Nexis. The earliest occurrence there is *Newsweek,* August 13, 1979, quoting William Goldman's Hollywood novel, *Tinsel.* The next occurrence is the *New York Times,* November 6, 1981: "Darryl Zanuck used to tell film makers, 'If you're in trouble, cut to the chase.' " Other early occurrences are also from movie contexts. It seems clear that this is a modern phrase referring to chase scenes in movies.

Fred R. Shapiro
Associate Librarian for Public Services
Yale Law School
New Haven, CT

 Just a follow-up to my *cut to the chase* question a couple of weeks ago. If you remember, I wanted to know the origin of the expression. With the help of some friends, I verified what everyone thought. In the 1994 *Random House Historical Dictionary of American Slang,* under *chase,* not *cut,* one finds the following:

[orig. ref. to chase scenes in action movies] get to the point; get on with it.

The first citation given is a literal use in a 1929 script ("Jannings escapes. . . . Cut to chase.").

John Stierman
Reference Librarian
Western Illinois University
Macomb, IL

□ □ □

Why a Handbasket?

 What does the expression *going to Hell in a handbasket* mean, and where does it come from?

Chana Lajcher
Reference Librarian
Jerusalem College of Technology
Jerusalem, Israel

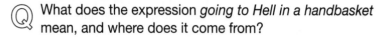 Bartlett J. Whiting, *Modern Proverbs and Proverbial Sayings* has an entry for "To go to Hell in a handbasket" (also in a wheelbarrow, on a shingle, in a handcart, on a sled, in a hack, etc.). The earliest citation given is J. Tully, *Beggars* (1926): "Country's bound for hell in a handbasket." There is no explanation as to the meaning of the phrase. Maybe the meaning is "going to Hell fast," although I don't know that handbaskets are especially fast.

Fred R. Shapiro
Associate Librarian for Public Services
Yale Law School
New Haven, CT

 A query by Chana Lajcher in 1994 asked about the meaning and origin of the expression *going to hell in a handbasket.* There were some good answers back then, but I have now found an excellent discussion by Jesse Sheidlower. Sheidlower, an editor at Random House and compiler of the definitive tome *The F-Word,* produces a

"Jesse's Word of the Day" feature for the Random House Web site. The June 29, 1996, "Jesse's Word of the Day" had this to say:

Well, you have to get there *somehow*, don't you? And a *handbasket* has the advantage of alliteration, always important when it comes to this sort of phrase.

Simple but pungent expressions [like "go to hell"] often develop elaborate variants. For example, the imprecation "kiss my ass!" can be expanded (from one direction) into "kiss my royal Irish ass!" or (from another) into "kiss my ass in Macy's window!" Similarly, the expression "go to hell" developed a number of variants describing the conveyance for reaching Pluto's realm, and these conveyances don't necessarily make sense. Carl Sandburg, writing about the 1890s, comments, "The first time I heard about a man 'going to hell in a hanging basket' I did a lot of wondering what a hanging basket is like." Whatever a "hanging basket" is, it gives us the alliteration, like such other common examples as "going to hell in a hack [i.e. a taxicab]," "handcart," and our "handbasket." Nonalliterating versions include "in a wheelbarrow," "on a poker," "in a bucket" ("But at least I'm enjoying the ride," as the Grateful Dead say), and "in a basket."

Fred R. Shapiro
Associate Librarian for Public Services
Yale Law School
New Haven, CT

□ □ □

Buying the Farm

 We are able to find the origin of the slang term *to buy (it)* meaning "to die," but does anyone know why or where "the farm" was added to the phrase?

Hedy N. R. Hustedde
Information Librarian
Bettendorf Public Library
Bettendorf, IA

The *Random House Historical Dictionary of American Slang,* which is now the definitive source for information on slang, gives the following information: The word *buy* had a sense of "to be charged for as a result of damaging, losing, etc.," dating back at least to 1938. In allusion to this sense, the expression *buy the farm* or variants thereof arose, especially in U.S. Air Force usage, meaning "(of a pilot or airplane) to crash." The first citations are two 1954 examples of *bought a plot* or *bought the shop.*

In 1955 the journal *American Speech* defined "buy the farm; buy a plot" as follows: "Crash fatally. (Jet pilots say that when a jet crashes on a farm the farmer usually sues the government for damages done to his farm by the crash, and the amount demanded is always more than enough to pay off the mortgage and then buy the farm outright. Since this type of crash is nearly always fatal to the pilot, the pilot pays for the farm with his life.)"

Fred R. Shapiro
Associate Librarian for Public Services
Yale Law School
New Haven, CT

Pushing the Envelope

 What is the source (documented, if possible) of the phrase *pushing the envelope,* meaning "approaching safe limits or operating parameters"?

 William Safire discussed the phrase *pushing the envelope* in his "On Language" columns in the *New York Times* of May 15 and June 26, 1988. In the first column, Safire said his earliest citation was *Aviation Week & Space Technology,* July 3, 1978, but that the phrase was popularized by Tom Wolfe's *The Right Stuff* (1979). Wolfe told Safire he first heard it in 1972 among test pilots: "They were speaking of the performance capabilities of an airplane as an envelope, as if there were a boundary." Safire pointed out that the *Oxford English Dictionary* records aeronautical meanings of the word *envelope,* i.e., "the gas or air container of a balloon or airship," later extended to mean optimum flight performance of any kind of aircraft. These meanings are recorded as early as 1901 and 1944 respectively.

In Safire's second column he reports responses by readers. One reader pointed out that in mathematics the envelope is the outer boundary of a related family of curves. Safire writes, "Number-crunchers in the aeronautical field applied this word to the limits of airplane operations."

Fred R. Shapiro
Associate Librarian for Public Services
Yale Law School
New Haven, CT

□ □ □

Who Is Murgatroyd?

Q Snagglepuss the Lion, the Hanna-Barbera cartoon character, often used the expression "Heavens to Murgatroyd!" Who is Murgatroyd?

A Bob Shar has pointed out that *Brewer's Dictionary of Names,* edited by Adrian Room, says this about Murgatroyd: "The name comes from Yorkshire, and represents an unidentified place-name that itself means 'Margaret's clearing', with the latter part of the name derived from the dialect word *royd,* 'clearing'."

Brewer's, however, is incorrect: there is only one locality in Yorkshire named Murgatroyd, and it is located in the West Riding, in what was formerly the manor of Wakefield. The name dates from at least the early fourteenth century, when it appears in the Wakefield manorial court rolls. As a graduate student in the mid-1970s I undertook a detailed study of the surviving court rolls prior to 1350, and remember seeing the name. So far as I and my colleagues at the Yorkshire Archaeological Society could determine at that time, *all* families bearing the surname Murgatroyd can be traced to individuals living in the vicinity of this locality. The manor of Wakefield is quite large, and I do not remember the precise location of Murgatroyd—I *think* it is in the parish of Halifax. In any case, A[lbert] H[ugh] Smith, *The Place-Names of the West Riding of Yorkshire,* English Place-Name Society, vols. 30–37 will give the precise location.

As to the *who* of "Heavens to Murgatroyd," if the phrase is not original to Hanna-Barbera, I am inclined to look for a mid- to late-nineteenth-century literary origin. Wilde is the obvious candidate, although it is certainly not in *The Importance of Being Earnest,* and it doesn't seem quite right for *Lady Windermere's Fan, A Woman of No Importance,* or *An Ideal Husband.* Another possibility is Sir William Schwenk Gilbert. In this century, Agatha Christie names a character in one of her novels Murgatroyd, but the character is murdered and can thus hardly be considered the source of a humorous exclamation. The expression is also not local Yorkshire humor, since the word *Murgatroyd,* which impinges so delightfully upon the sensibilities of the average American (and of the inhabitants of southern England), is known to the inhabitants of the West Riding as a local place-name and seems no more silly to them than, say, the word "Albany" does to the average New Yorker.

Michael Palmer
Consultant Archivist
Claremont, CA

Responding to Michael Palmer's suggestion of W. S. Gilbert as the source of the *Murgatroyd* in "Heavens to Murgatroyd!": the Gilbert and Sullivan operetta *Ruddigore* revolves around the melodramatic villainies of Sir Ruthven Murgatroyd and Sir Despard Murgatroyd, who are forced by a family curse to commit one evil act per day. I'm not sure how this applies to Snagglepuss, unless one of the writers for Hanna-Barbera saw *Ruddigore* at a formative age and simply thought the name was funny. Documenting the connection would be difficult.

John Maxstadt
Public Services Librarian
Lamar University
Orange, TX

 According to *Brewer's Quotations,* "A cartoon lion called Snagglepuss, which came out of the Hanna-Barbera studios in the 1960s, was given to exclaiming 'Heavens to Murgatroyd!' He made his first appearance in *The Yogi Bear Show,* but this catchphrase was apparently not original. An American correspondent noted (1993): 'It was a favorite expression of a favorite uncle of mine in the 1940s, and my wife also remembers it from her growing-up years in the '40s.' "

Fred R. Shapiro
Associate Librarian for Public Services
Yale Law School
New Haven, CT

Holy Toledo!

 A patron called today wanting to know the origins of the phrase *holy Toledo.* We tried several dictionaries *(Oxford English Dictionary,* unabridged *Webster's, Dictionary of American Slang, Origin of Everyday Phrases, Dictionary of Americanisms)* and found:

holy cow

holy Moses

holy shit

a variety of other holy items

but unfortunately not *holy Toledo.* We theorize it could perhaps have some connection to Toledo, Spain, since (having been there) we think Toledo, Ohio, particularly unlikely, but we remain in the dark.

Jamie McGrath
Senior Librarian
Alameda Free Library Reference Department
Alameda, CA

 We had this as a rush question and called the Toledo Public Library for their wisdom on this matter. Here is what they said:

The origins of the phrase are obscure. There are six speculations:

1. It is a sarcastic term criticizing Toledo for having more saloons than churches.

2. It refers to the holy city of Toledo, Spain.

3. Gangsters in the 1920s and 1930s used it because Toledo police were lenient toward safe crackers and rumrunners as long as they behaved while they were in town.

4. Vaudeville performers always spoke of the poor business during Holy Week (the week of Easter). Attendance at vaudeville shows was so poor in Toledo that every week was Holy Week—ergo "holy Toledo."

5. There are many churches on Collingwood Avenue.

6. Billy Sunday once referred to the city as "holy Toledo" during a revival meeting in 1908 in Toledo.

Jessica Bowen
BALIS Reference Center
San Francisco Public Library
San Francisco, CA

X Marks the Generation

What does the X stand for in *Generation X*?

Generation X was originally a 1970s punk band (that's where Billy Idol got his start). Probably the name was a takeoff of the Richard Hell and the Voidoids song "Blank Generation" and other punk messages of nihilism and alienation. Later, *Generation X* was used as a book title. Then the media picked up on it (basically as a marketing tool) as a term for those who are sometimes referred to as "twenty-somethings."

Chuck Cody
Reference Librarian
Columbus Metropolitan Library
Columbus, OH

Actually, the term is older than Billy Idol's band. Charles Hamblett published a book titled *Generation X* in 1964, about the disaffected British youth of that time. Douglas Coupland popularized the term in his 1991 novel, *Generation X: Tales for an Accelerated Culture.*

Fred R. Shapiro
Associate Librarian for Public Services
Yale Law School
New Haven, CT

Ain't No Free Lunch

 Does anyone know the origin of TANSTAAFL, There ain't no such thing as a free lunch.

The earliest thing I have seen it in was a Robert Heinlein book, *The Moon Is a Harsh Mistress.* No luck with *Bartlett's, Peter's,* or *Oxford English Dictionary.*

Susan L. Benzer
(formerly) Research Librarian
Phillips Laboratory Research Library
Hanscom Air Force Base, MA
(currently) WEBnet Consortium Administrator
Babson College
Babson Park, MA

 The earliest known usage of "There ain't no such thing as a free lunch" is an editorial by Walter Morrow titled "The Fable of the King and All the Wise Men—or Economics in Eight Words," in the *San Francisco News,* June 1, 1949, p. 14. In Morrow's fable, a king asks his advisers to summarize economics in a "short and simple text." After they initially respond with eighty-seven volumes of six hundred pages each, the king's wrath and resulting executions force the economists to restate their science in ever-briefer summations. Finally, the last economist produces an eight-word distillation: "There ain't no such thing as free lunch." The editorial is apparently a reprint of a 1938 editorial in the same newspaper.

Fred R. Shapiro
Associate Librarian for Public Services
Yale Law School
New Haven, CT

□ □ □

Till the Fat Lady Sings

Q "The opera ain't over until the fat lady sings." We have citations to Dick Motta and Dan Cook, dating to about 1978. However, our patron says she remembers using the phrase long before that, so she wants to find earlier citations. Can anyone oblige?

Judy Lane
Reference Coordinator
Mountain-Valley Library System
Sacramento, CA

A Ralph Keyes, in his 1992 book *Nice Guys Finish Seventh,* devotes a good bit of a chapter titled "Poor Richard's Plagiarism" to shooting down the notion that "the opera ain't over till the fat lady sings" was actually coined by either Motta or Dan Cook. Motta never claimed the quote.

"Dan Cook," writes Keyes, "may simply have been taking part in a great Southern tradition: foisting off shopworn Dixieisms on unsuspecting Yankees as fresh merchandise. An obscure 1976 booklet called *Southern Words and Sayings* included this entry: 'Church ain't out 'till the fat lady sings.' "

"Alvin Bethard of the Dupre Library in Lafayette, Louisiana," Keyes continues, "said that this was the way he'd always heard that saying while growing up in central Louisiana in the 1950s and 1960s."

Keyes names various other "longtime Southerners"— including a San Antonio physician, a television newscaster from Charlotte (Bob Inman, who recalled hearing "it ain't over till the fat lady sings" when he was secretary to Alabama Governor Albert Brewer in the late 1960s), a political reporter (Bob Ingraham), who said he first heard the "opera ain't . . ." in a context he couldn't recall, while working for the *Montgomery Advertiser* in the 1950s. (I was personally saddened that he did not cite Uncle Bubba's Aunt Sadie, but I'll get over it . . .)

Keyes doesn't do anything to actually pin down the origin, but he does emphatically back up Judy Lane's patron.

Bob Shar
Humanities Librarian
Forsyth County Public Library
Winston-Salem, NC

It Takes a Stumpers to Answer a Query

 I'm looking for the origin of the saying, "It takes a village to raise a child." Any ideas???

Cathy Burnstead
Public Services Librarian
Juneau Public Library
Juneau, AK

Albert Scheven, *Swahili Proverbs,* #474, p. 123:

"MKONO MMOJA HAULEI MWANA."

"One hand cannot bring up a child (or, cannot nurse a child). Child upbringing is a communal effort."

Scheven, who was a missionary in Tanzania, cites his source as S. S. Farsi, *Swahili Sayings from Zanzibar,* Vol. 1, *Proverbs.*

Sue Watkins
Internet Research Specialist
Las Vegas, NV

Fish Find

Q What is the provenance of the quotation, "Give a man a fish, and you feed him for a day. Teach a man to fish, and you feed him for a lifetime."

A We, too, have had the fish quote at our library. We found a reference to it in *RQ*, winter 1978, p. 184. The following is quoted from that.

According to R. T. Tripp's *International Thesaurus of Quotations* [1970] (p. 646), it is a Chinese proverb. SCAN librarians also located a version in J. J. Servan-Schreiber's *The American Challenge* [verso of title page]:

> *If you give a man a fish,*
> *He will have a single meal.*
> *If you teach him how to fish,*
> *He will eat all his life.*

The quotation is attributed to the "Kuantzu, a philosophical work of ancient (possibly fourth century B.C.) China."

Deb Palmer
Reference Librarian
Cedar Rapids Public Library
Cedar Rapids, IA

☐ ☐ ☐

Emerson Didn't Say Everything

Q A patron is looking for a citation for the source of the following quotation, attributed to Ralph Waldo Emerson:

> *To laugh often and much;*
> *To win the respect of intelligent people,*
> *And the affections of children;*
> *To earn the appreciation of honest critics*
> *And endure the betrayal of false friends;*
> *To appreciate beauty;*
> *To leave the world a bit better,*
> *Whether by a healthy child,*

A garden patch,
Or a redeemed social condition;
To know even one life has breathed easier
Because you have lived:
This is to have succeeded.

Although it is laid out in this format in the patron's source, I don't think it is actually poetry but reformatted prose. It has been quoted in a number of places: Dear Abby's column, several scholarly and popular articles—but never with a citation that would tell which of Emerson's works was the source.

We have checked concordances to Emerson's poetry and to five essays, various quotation books, *Granger's Index,* and some online sources (in the hope that we would find a proper citation to the quote in a scholarly article that included it). No luck.

Stacy Pober
Information Alchemist
Manhattan College Libraries
Riverdale, NY

 The quotation, often titled "Success," is *not* by Emerson. It was written by Bessie A. Stanley of Lincoln, Kansas. She received an award of $250 for it in November 1905, from the George Livingston Richards Co. of Boston. Various versions have appeared in newspapers, but according to her son, Judge Arthur J. Stanley, the correct version is the one given in the eleventh (1937) edition of Bartlett's *Familiar Quotations.*

Sources for the above include a reply published in *Notes and Queries,* July 1976, p. 312; *Modern Women,* 1905; and, of all things, Ann Landers, *Gems,* p. 42.

Charles Anderson
Editor, "The Exchange," RQ
(Reference and User Services Quarterly,
a publication of the American Library Association)
Bellevue, WA

□ □ □

Set It Free

 What is the complete text and origin of this popular quote:

"If you love something set it free. If it comes back it's yours, if it doesn't it never was . . ."

 I remember seeing this on bumper stickers, but don't remember the exact wording. What I do remember, though, is the bumper sticker that read, "If you love something, set it free. If it doesn't come back to you, hunt it down and kill it."

Sorry.

Ruth A. Frear
Sonoma, CA

 Tad Tuleja says:

The 1960s, which gave us "It's cool" and "Whatever turns you on" and "Let it be," also gave us pop guru Jess Lair's wonderfully flaccid ode to self-determination. From his 1974 book *I Ain't Much, Baby—But I'm All I Got,* it goes like this:

> *If you want something very very badly,*
> *let it go free. If it comes back to you*
> *it's yours forever. If it doesn't, it was*
> *never yours to begin with.*

—Source: Tuleja, Tad. *Quirky Quotations,* p. 158.

In chapter 20 of his book, Jess Lair tells how he had his students in the school of education at Montana State University write comments, questions, or feelings on index cards and turn them in voluntarily and anonymously if they chose. The writing on the cards did not have to be original; quotations did not have to be attributed. Lair lists many of his students' card writings, mostly aphorisms.

Our quarry appears in the "Juniors and Seniors" section:

If you want something very, very badly, let it go free. If it comes back to you, it's yours forever. If it doesn't, it was never yours to begin with.

—Source: Jess Lair, *I Ain't Much, Baby—But I'm All I've Got,* chapter 20, "Our Magic Cards," p. 203.

So, it looks as though the originator was a college junior or senior, unless the student copied it from a book, periodical, greeting card, bumper sticker, show card, refrigerator magnet, poster, restroom wall . . .

Bill Thomas
Reference Librarian
County of Los Angeles Public Library
Lancaster, CA

□ □ □

Corrupt Youth, Corrupt Quotation

 What is the source of the classical Greek or Roman quotation about youth being undisciplined?

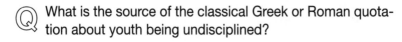 This sounds like a version of what reference librarians refer to as the "Socrates" (or even sometimes the "Hitler") quote. Usually it appears as follows:

The children now love luxury; they have bad manners, contempt for authority; they show discourtesy for elders and love chatter in place of exercise. Children are now tyrants, not the servants of their households. They no longer rise when elders enter the room. They contradict their parents, chatter before company, gobble up dainties at the table, cross their legs, and tyrannize their teachers.

Ralph Keyes talks about it in his *Nice Guys Finish Seventh*, p. 20. It's appeared a number of times in "The Exchange" in *RQ*, with no one ever establishing that it was a real quotation.

Charles Anderson
Editor, "The Exchange," RQ
(Reference and User Services Quarterly,
a publication of the American Library Association)
Bellevue, WA

□ □ □

Different Strokes

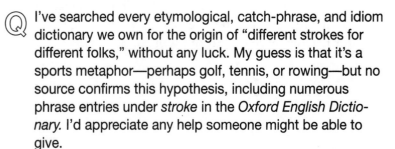 I've searched every etymological, catch-phrase, and idiom dictionary we own for the origin of "different strokes for different folks," without any luck. My guess is that it's a sports metaphor—perhaps golf, tennis, or rowing—but no source confirms this hypothesis, including numerous phrase entries under *stroke* in the *Oxford English Dictionary.* I'd appreciate any help someone might be able to give.

David Isaacson
Assistant Head of Reference and Humanities Librarian
Waldo Library
Western Michigan University
Kalamazoo, MI

 This is clearly proverbial. The *Dictionary of American Proverbs* (1992) includes it, but indicates that it did not appear in any earlier proverb dictionaries. The earliest occurrence I find in a search of Lexis/Nexis is in a 1973 New York court decision, *People v. Mature Enterprises,* 73 Misc. 2d 749, 343 N.Y.S. 2d 911 (1973). This case involved the obscenity of the film *Deep Throat,* suggesting a sexual origin for the word *stroke* in the proverb. However, most of the earliest usages on Nexis, dating from the late 1970s, are in nonsexual contexts.

My intuition is that this originated in African–American usage, and that it is much more likely to refer to a sexual meaning of *stroke* than to a sports meaning.

Fred R. Shapiro
Associate Librarian for Public Services
Yale Law School
New Haven, CT

 One use of the phrase "different strokes for different folks" that hasn't been mentioned here yet is this: in the 1969 number one hit "Everyday People" by Sly and the Family Stone, the refrain contains the words "different strokes for different folks."

Where are all the aging hippies on this list? How could we miss this one?

Kee Malesky
Reference Librarian
National Public Radio
Washington, DC

 A little more support for my conjecture that "different strokes for different folks" originated in African–American usage: Robert L. Chapman, *New Dictionary of American Slang,* says it is "fr black." Rosalind Ferguson, *Shorter Dictionary of Catch Phrases,* says "orig used by US Blacks, the phrase had entered general usage by around 1970." Kee Malesky's posting, pointing out that the phrase was used in the song "Everyday People" by Sly and the Family Stone in 1969, also tends to support this hypothesis.

Fred R. Shapiro
Associate Librarian for Public Services
Yale Law School
New Haven, CT

No Cigar

Q This is one of those "Oh, this question will only take a minute," but then the wretched thing refuses to be found! Can anyone supply the source for the humorous quote "close, but no cigar!"? I have tried many of the standard quotations sources under "cigar," to no avail. Does anyone have a dictionary of show business quotations? The thoughts are that the source could be Groucho Marx or W. C. Fields . . .

Pamela Spooner
Reference Librarian
Southwest Texas State University
San Marcos, TX

A "The Exchange," *RQ*, fall 1984, vol. 24, no. 1, carried this note:

From William Safire's column "On Language" in the *New York Times Magazine* (April 6, 1980, p. 10) comes the answer to the query about the origin of the expression "close but no cigar!" (*RQ* 23, Spring 1984, p. 271): "It stems from carnival use. As a test of strength, the contestant swung a sledgehammer to drive an arrow up a pole and win the prize of a cigar. When the arrow failed to reach the top and ring the bell, the barker would gleefully commiserate: 'close—but no cigar!' " Both BARC and Eddie Hoffman of SCAN (Southern California Answering Network) sent this answer.

Charles Anderson
Editor, "The Exchange," RQ
(Reference and User Services Quarterly,
a publication of the American Library Association)
Bellevue, WA

A According to *A Dictionary of Catch Phrases: American and British, from the Sixteenth Century to the Present Day* by Eric Partridge, revised and updated edition, " 'Close, but no cigar' is a US catch phrase, used mostly in sporting contests; since c. 1930. Probably from a cigar often being presented to the winner of some minor competition."

Partridge compares this to the British expression "give the gentleman a coconut," which originated at the coconut-shy booth at the fairgrounds. The player threw a ball at coconuts. When he knocked the coconuts off with the ball, the call was, "Give the gentleman a coconut."

Carol A. Singer
Librarian
National Agricultural Library
Washington, DC

In Jonathan E. Lighter's *Random House Historical Dictionary of American Slang* (a sensational reference work that all reference librarians should know and treasure!), "close, but no cigar" is listed under *cigar*. The earliest citation given there is from the 1935 film *Annie Oakley:* "Close, Colonel, but no cigar!" It also lists 1938 and 1940 quotations from John O'Hara novels, along with later examples. No other historical dictionary, proverb dictionary, or quotation dictionary appears to have any better information.

Fred R. Shapiro
Associate Librarian for Public Services
Yale Law School
New Haven, CT

□ □ □

Moccasins Mystery

Does anyone know the origin of the saying about "walking a mile in another man's moccasins" to understand his problems? We've checked the usual books of quotations—about nine or ten—without success.

Joyce Fellows Murphy
Reference Specialist
Mid-York Library System
Utica, NY

I checked back files of "The Exchange." As I suspected, there is no definitive attribution that any readers have ever sent in. It has been found on a leaflet published by the St. Francis Indian Mission in St. Francis, South Dakota. A Rev. R. M. Demeyer, S.J., from the mission wrote back in 1974 that the prayer "is traditional among the Indian people, especially in the northern plains." He went on to note that "mile" is not to be found in the Indian vocabulary, instead the word "day" or "moon" is usually how it appears.

Stephen A. Langone, a specialist in American Indian affairs at the Library of Congress, has never found any better information. The Indian Committee of the National Council of Churches uses it, calling it a traditional Indian saying. It has also been attributed to the Sioux Indians and to Chief Joseph of the Nez Percé Indians.

Charles Anderson
Editor, "The Exchange," RQ
(Reference and User Services Quarterly,
a publication of the American Library Association)
Bellevue, WA

Been There . . .

 Does anyone claim to be the first person to have said, "Been there . . . done that"? We have a patron who is looking for the origins of this rather too often used phrase.

We have tried all the usual sources for quotes and phrases, to no effect.

Bob Schuler
Tacoma Public Library
Tacoma, WA

The earliest citation I have for this phrase is from *Sports Illustrated,* February 9, 1987: "Conner, as the Aussies say, has 'been there, done that.' "

Fred R. Shapiro
Associate Librarian for Public Services
Yale Law School
New Haven, CT

 A couple of months ago I responded to the query about the origins of "been there, done that" with a 1987 *Sports Illustrated* usage suggesting that this is an Australianism. Now there is further evidence pointing to an Australian origin: In today's *New York Times,* William Safire reports a citation supplied to him by wombat David Barnhart. David found in the *Macquarie Dictionary of New Words* an October 21, 1983, usage of "been there, done that" in the *Union Recorder,* published at the University of Sydney.

Fred R. Shapiro
Associate Librarian for Public Services
Yale Law School
New Haven, CT

Kill What Messenger?

 Does anyone know the source of the phrase "don't kill the messenger"?

Kathleen Milford
Assistant Director of Development
University of Texas M. D. Anderson Cancer Center
Houston, TX

 I searched the quotation dictionaries, proverb dictionaries, and word and phrase dictionaries in a major research library's reference collection, and it appears that "kill the messenger" is one of those proverbial phrases that, although quite common, has eluded the dictionaries. Thus there is no authoritative answer as to where it originated. The closest I can find is Stevenson's *Home Book of Proverbs,* which quotes "Messengers should neither be headed nor hanged" from David Ferguson, *Scottish Proverbs,* p. 76 (c. 1595). Stevenson further notes, "cited by Kelly, *Scottish Proverbs,* p. 246, with the comment, 'An excuse for carrying an ungrateful message.' "

The earliest example of the exact phrase that I have found is the following: An RLIN search pulls up a 1970 book title by William J. Small, *To Kill a Messenger: Television News and the Real World.*

Fred R. Shapiro
Associate Librarian for Public Services
Yale Law School
New Haven, CT

 More on "kill the messenger": Stevenson's *Home Book of Proverbs* also quotes Sophocles' *Antigone,* "No man delights in the bearer of bad news" and "The bearer of dread tidings need must quake." Stevenson also quotes an anonymous French source (c. 1250), "Misfortune comes all too quickly to the bearer of bad news."

Suzanne Fisher has pointed out that this question has appeared in "The Exchange" in *RQ.* I quote the Spring 1990 "Exchange": "This theme has been found from Greek drama to Chinese and Scottish proverbs to Shakespeare, but no first use has been identified. . . . The Biblical story of David killing the man who brought the news of Saul's death is often cited as a source, but the messenger was killed because he boasted of killing Saul himself."

Fred R. Shapiro
Associate Librarian for Public Services
Yale Law School
New Haven, CT

□ □ □

Desiderata

Q Several weeks ago, someone inquired about a piece entitled "Desiderata." I don't recall seeing any kind of an
attempt at answering the inquiry, and I have purged the
original note from my files. It seems that the inquiry
concerned the authorship of the piece.

If the "Desiderata" in question is the rather familiar piece in
which part of the meaning is that one should endeavor to
live at peace with oneself, one's creator, one's fellow
beings, and the whole of creation, it is probably an anonymous work. The one I'm thinking of is occasionally
published in newspapers and other periodicals. If this is,
indeed, the "Desiderata" in question, I am sending out the
following citation from our catalog, which may be of some
help:

————. DESIDERATA: FOUND IN OLD SAINT PAUL'S
CHURCH, BALTIMORE, DATED 1692. Leicester: New Broom
Press, 1972.

Surprisingly, we have this twelve-page book in our rare
books collection; so it cannot be lent via interlibrary loan
from the University of Georgia Libraries. You could, of
course, check OCLC to see whether it's available elsewhere. (We probably have it in our special collections
because it contains fine artwork or is a limited private
press edition.)

I have a newspaper clipping of the "Desiderata" in my
personal files that I can photocopy and send you, if you'd
like. I think the newspaper clipping states that the original
piece is an engraving on a stone tablet at St. Paul's
Church. If memory serves me correctly, the clipping further
states that the "Desiderata" is thought to be the work of an
anonymous author. I don't have the clipping in front of me,
and I don't consider newspaper clippings to be necessarily

authoritative sources, so this information would require
verification.

Jay Evatt
Reference Department
University of Georgia Libraries
Athens, GA

 The residents of Terre Haute, Indiana, who had a centen-
nial celebration to honor Max Ehrmann, the author of
"Desiderata," would probably be appalled to hear that the
myth of the "Old St. Paul's" was still being given as a
source for this material. You might want to check out *The
Desiderata of Happiness; a Collection of Philosophical Poems,* by
Max Ehrmann (several editions), as well as discussions in
"The Exchange" 11:67; 363–65; 12:392–93.

Charles Anderson
Editor, "The Exchange," RQ
(Reference and User Services Quarterly,
a publication of the American Library Association)
Bellevue, WA

 In addition to the other stuff in the Stumpers Archives
about "Desiderata," you can find it in *Respectfully Quoted*
(p. 212). This gives the source as *The Poems of Max
Ehrmann,* p. 165 (1948).

Joy Tillotson
Information Services Librarian
Queen Elizabeth II Library
Memorial University of Newfoundland
St. John's, Newfoundland
Canada

Random Kindness

What is the origin of the slogan "Practice random acts of
kindness and senseless beauty"?

The phrase "Practice random kindness and senseless acts of beauty" was written by Anne Herbert, a writer in Berkeley, California, in 1982. Herbert is a peace activist who first published the phrase in an alternative magazine called the *CoEvolution Quarterly*—now named the *Whole Earth Review.* The slogan was popularized in May 1991 when a San Francisco columnist named Adair Lara wrote about Herbert and her "random kindness." The article was picked up in *Reader's Digest* and on e-mail. It suddenly began appearing on posters, coffee mugs, etc.

Herbert states that the "acts of kindness" should be done anonymously without expectations for a thank you or a reward.

Susan Midland
Librarian
Chrysler Museum of Art
Norfolk, VA

Book of Phantom Sorrows

Q In Dean Koontz's *Midnight* the following quote appears at
the beginning of part one: "Where eerie figures caper to
some midnight music that only they can hear."—*The Book
of Counted Sorrows.*

A student is trying to locate *The Book of Counted Sorrows.*
We have checked WorldCat without success. Any assis-
tance would be appreciated.

Bruce Johnson
Reference Services Coordinator
University of Wisconsin–Parkside
Kenosha, WI

A Back in April 1989, we received the first of several queries
about Dean Koontz's *Book of Counted Sorrows.* At that
time, Mr. Koontz was listed in the Orange County, California, telephone book. (He has since gotten an unlisted
number.) I called him, and he told me that it was his own
apocryphal invention. Whenever he can't find a fitting
little ditty to illustrate his works, he makes one up and
attributes it to the nonexistent *Book of Counted Sorrows.* At
that time he had no plans to publish this phantom poetry
book. We have not heard of its subsequent publication to
date, but maybe someday. . . .

Shari I. Haber
Reference Librarian
Metropolitan Cooperative Library System
Pasadena, CA

□ □ □

Editing with a Heavy Hand

 Q A patron wants to know the names of a handful of writers whose wives destroyed a portion of their work.

Brack Stovall
Library Assistant—Electronic Reference
Montgomery-Floyd Regional Libraries
Blacksburg Branch
Blacksburg, VA

 A According to folk history/legend, Sequoia's first version of the Cherokee system of writing was burned by his wife, and he had to reconstruct it over a period of years.

L. Jeanne Powers
Reference Librarian
Bristol Public Library
Bristol, VA/TN

 A There's Hemingway's first wife, who lost an original manuscript (only copy) on a train.

Rosy Brewer
Reference Librarian
Monterey Bay Cooperative Library System (MOBAC)
Monterey, CA

 A Isabel, wife of Sir Richard Burton (*Arabian Nights* and Middle East and Africa explorer) destroyed some of his writings after his death rather than publish them, because she judged them "unseemly."

Martha Ann (Matt) Mueller
Scholes Library of Ceramics
NYS College of Ceramics at Alfred University
Alfred, NY

 A I know you specified "wives," but if you want to expand this to surviving family, I believe Emily Dickinson qualifies. Her family kept, "edited," and, I believe, destroyed much correspondence and poetry that did not fit the image of Dickinson that they were trying to create. The

Bloomsbury Guide to Women's Literature and *Magill's Survey of American Literature* both have good articles on her.

Mary Pauli
Reference Librarian
Clackamas County Library
Oak Grove, OR

10 Music

Theremin Thoughts

 Our patron wants instructions for building a "thurmin." He has lost his copy of instructions that he said were printed in the sixties or seventies in *Popular Mechanics.*

Unfortunately, neither the word "thurmin" nor any variation that I can come up with is listed in any current *Reader's Guide,* nor in any dictionary.

He describes the thurmin as an electronic instrument, sort of like a radio component. On one side is an antenna, and on the other side is a loop. If you move your hand near or up and down the antenna, you can regulate the tone. If you move your hand near the loop, you can change the volume.

He says that this instrument was used to make background music for "weird" science fiction movies. I have checked everything, even the Stumpers Archives (I was a good girl). But our *Reader's Guides* do not go back that far, and our copy of the *Popular Mechanics Do-It-Yourself* encyclopedia is missing the "T" volume.

Any leads would be given utmost thanks.

Reita Fackerell
Library Director
Seaside Public Library
Seaside, OR

 The word is "theremin"—I'm pretty sure of that spelling. Its most famous uses were in the soundtrack of the movie

Spellbound and the Beach Boys' greatest-of-all-greatest hits, "Good Vibrations."

Lois Aleta Fundis
Reference Librarian
Mary H. Weir Public Library
Weirton, WV

 If anyone is interested in about ninety minutes of this stuff . . . watch the late-fifties classic sci-fi film *Forbidden Planet* (featuring a young, pre-absurd Leslie Nielsen). It is wall-to-wall exotic theremin music.

Kurt W. Wagner
Reference Librarian
Sarah Byrd Askew Library
William Paterson University of New Jersey
Wayne, NJ

 The terrific movie *Ed Wood* has a very interesting score, mostly composed by Howard Shore. Shore makes extensive use of the theremin in his score, and it's available on CD. A big hit of last year's New York and Sundance film festivals is a movie called *Theremin: An Electronic Odyssey.*

Jim Hunt
Associate Professor
Business and Online Search Specialist
University Library
California State University
Dominguez Hills, CA

 Do some subjects just float out there waiting to be found? Today as I was checking in periodicals I came across an article in the May 1995 issue of *Electronic Musician* (pp. 58–63) titled "Build the EM Optical Theremin."

Judy Mowrey
Librarian
De Anza College
Cupertino, CA

□ □ □

Hokey History

Looking for information on the history and origin of the "Hokey Pokey" (song and dance). I've been able to piece the following together: It is an adaptation of the "Looby Loo," and it originated in England during World War II. Originally, it was called the "Cokey Cokey"; it has also been known as "Hokey Cokey."

Terry Simas
Reference Coordinator
North State Cooperative Library System
Willows, CA

The Jacksonville, Florida, paper had a short article about the death of the author of the "Hokey Pokey" on April 11, 1996, at the age of eighty-three in Boise, Idaho. According to the article, the "Hokey Pokey" was written by Larry LaPrise (born Roland Lawrence LaPrise), a native of Detroit and a postal worker in Idaho, in the late 1940s. He wrote it for the "après ski" crowd at Sun Valley, but never made any real money on it or received the credit that he deserved. The credit for the first recording of the song was given to the Ram Trio in 1949. The report commented on the fact that nearly everyone thinks that the song and its actions are folklore, and that is one of the reasons that LaPrise never got the recognition that he deserved. (The article was accompanied by a picture of LaPrise, probably from the late 1940s or early 1950s from the look of it.)

Beth Bojack
Reference Librarian
John B. Coleman Library
Prairie View A&M University
Prairie View, TX

Larry LaPrise, who claimed it was his invention, died April 4, 1996. Several war veterans called the AP protesting that they knew the song and dance before LaPrise claimed to have invented it in 1949. A December 1945 article in *Dance Magazine* corroborates the veterans' recollection of a craze sweeping England at the time. All of this is related in an AP news story by Mitchell Landsberg dated April 14, 1996.

T. F. Mills
Serials Librarian
University of Denver Library
Denver, CO

 Anyone who claims to have invented the hokey-pokey (or hokey-cokey) in 1949 is wrong. I can remember being taken to the local football oval to dance the hokey-pokey (and revel in other ways) on the night World War II ended in 1945, and it was not new then.

Katherine Cummings
Reference Librarian
Macquarie University
Sydney, New South Wales
Australia

 Further to my reminiscences of dancing the hokey-pokey on V-J (now V-P) night in 1945, I have now checked the *Oxford English Dictionary,* 2nd edition, and find a 1943 reference under *hokey-cokey* that runs:

hokey-cokey [cf. hokee-pokee] A kind of dance.

1943 *Dancing Times* Sept. 570/2 I found a party-dance called the "Hokey Pokey" . . . the correct name is "Cokey Cokey" . . . the chorus runs: . . . "You do the Cokey Cokey and you turn around That's what it's all about."

Katherine Cummings
Reference Librarian
Macquarie University
Sydney, New South Wales
Australia

One Tune Fits All

I haven't seen *Legends of the Fall,* but based on TV previews, am perplexed by the fact that the film appears to use music that is identical to the music in *Last of the Mohicans.* I have never noted this in any other movie, other than classical themes being repeated or previously used music being employed in a satirical or ironic way. What is the explanation?

Fred R. Shapiro
Associate Librarian for Public Services
Yale Law School
New Haven, CT

Yes, Fred R. Shapiro, I've noticed the exact same thing. . . .

I especially liked the score to *Last of the Mohicans,* so I did recognize its use in this and other ads for other movies. If/when you see the film in question, you'll notice that they don't use the score you heard in the ads. In other words, it's just an advertising ploy. "They" (the publicists) use music that is dramatic, lush, or whatever effect they're going for . . . and not necessarily something that actually comes from the film's score.

I've also noticed lots of use of the score from the *Gettysburg* movie—to promote other films, for emotional effect by news reporters, even in sports pieces! I suppose if they pay the copyright use fee, it's legal and ethical, but it can confuse film music fans.

Kee Malesky
Reference Librarian
National Public Radio
Washington, DC

The most common explanation for this phenomenon is that the music for the soon-to-be-released movie has not been composed yet, or at least has not been finally decided upon. Generally, the music is just about the last element to be added to the finished film, since the composer scores the scenes as they appear in the final edit. Apparently many, if not all, movie music composers prefer to wait until late in the editing process so that they have a good idea of what the finished film is going to look like. Since the composer's work is not yet complete when the trailers are distributed, the producers will choose some suitably dramatic music from some previous film (to which they have legal access). This also has the advantage of associating the coming movie, in a subliminal manner, with a prior "hit" in the audience's mind. I read an article about this some time back, so the above info is from memory.

Bill Lowe
Reference Librarian
Westminster College
Fulton, MO

 It's entirely possible that previews for *Legends of the Fall* are accompanied by the musical score from *Last of the Mohicans* or some other familiar sources.

In most circumstances, the musical score is the last thing to be incorporated into the final cut of the film. In terms of timing, this frequently creates logistical cliff-hangers for the producers, who advertise the availability of film titles for dates established well in advance. Previews are thus thrown together far ahead of the completed film and almost always use fragments from previous scores or existing musical sources, whether classical or popular. One piece of music is used so frequently in previews that I burst out laughing every time I hear it on the screen. It's Karl Orff's *Carmina Burana.* It is used once or twice each year to promote a major film. One that immediately comes to mind is Mel Gibson's *Hamlet.* The preview was pure *Carmina Burana,* but there was not one note of it included in the actual film. *Carmina Burana* and Richard

Strauss's *Thus Spake Zarathustra* (remember the theme from *2001*) are also used extensively in television commercials. Orff never made much money from his music. What a pity he didn't live long enough to reap this incredible commercial harvest! Then again, perhaps the artist in him would have rebelled against the commercialization.

Jim Hunt
Associate Professor
Business and Online Search Specialist
University Library
California State University
Dominguez Hills, CA

□   □   □

The Opera Ain't Over Till the Fat Lady Eats

 Here's a good one. We have a regular patron who recently learned that Chicken Tetrazzini was created and named after an opera singer, Louisa Tetrazzini. So now he wants to know if there are any other food dishes that were created/named after opera singers. Sounds like a long shot to me but if anyone knows, it will be someone in Stumperville.

Sue Baldwin
Supervising Librarian
Newport News Public Library System
Newport News, VA
(formerly of Norfolk Public Library, Norfolk, VA)

 Melba toast, peach Melba, and Melba sauce were all named after Australian soprano Nellie Melba.

Will White
Library Assistant
San Mateo County Library
San Mateo, CA

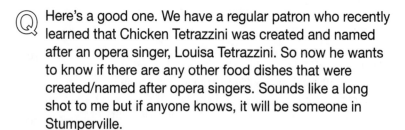 The *Morris Dictionary of Word and Phrase Origins* by William and Mary Morris has an entry "food from the opera." In

addition to chicken Tetrazzini, peach Melba, and Melba toast, it lists sauce Caruso (named for the famous tenor Enrico Caruso), which is marinara sauce with sauteed mushrooms and chicken livers added.

Will White
Library Assistant
San Mateo County Library
San Mateo, CA

□ □ □

Real Sloop

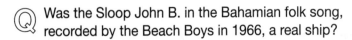 Was the Sloop John B. in the Bahamian folk song, recorded by the Beach Boys in 1966, a real ship?

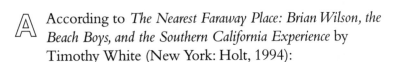 According to *The Nearest Faraway Place: Brian Wilson, the Beach Boys, and the Southern California Experience* by Timothy White (New York: Holt, 1994):

The song ["Sloop John B."] . . . [was] last heard on the Kingston Trio's album *From the Hungry i* in an adaptation by poet-folk archivist Carl Sandburg and Lee Hays of the Weavers. Also known as "John B. Sails," the song was a traditional shanty of the Bahamas, telling the saga of the ship's tragic grounding off Nassau as viewed through the bloodshot eyes of its unhappy crew. The remains of the ill-fated *John B.* lay undisturbed in the shoal at Governor's Harbor until they were excavated in 1926, and the publicity raised the popular profile of the commemorative ditty. (p. 260)

Sounds real to me.

Amy K. Blanchard
Adult Services Librarian
Vernon Area Public Library
Lincolnshire, IL

11 Art

Hidden Hand

Q What is the significance of Napoleon putting his hand in his jacket in portraits?

A In 1812 Jacques-Louis David painted *Napoleon in His Study*. Although David had painted Napoleon on numerous occasions, only in this last one of David's paintings of the emperor does he portray him with his hand stuck in his waistcoat. At least I didn't see that pose anywhere else in three books of David's paintings. And, I have also learned, Napoleon was not present for a sitting, nor did he commission the painting. David painted him using previous images, his memory, and his imagination; and he had great freedom in composing the portrait the way he wished. As a result, for this painting at least, it was David, not Bonaparte, who was responsible for sticking Napoleon's hand inside his clothing. (See Dorothy Johnson. *Jacques-Louis David: Art in Metamorphosis.* Johnson, however, never mentions the "characteristic pose.")

Here, it seems to me, are the next questions to ask:

Were there paintings or depictions of Napoleon in his "characteristic pose" before the painting of 1812? Was it this David painting that has significantly influenced the iconography of Napoleon; or was David, who had had some acquaintance with Napoleon, merely depicting a common mannerism Old Boney had previously displayed? Was a hand in a shirt or waistcoat characteristic of Napoleon, or was it a common pose in portraiture of the era?

The answers are, I haven't found out yet.

In an admittedly superficial search of the Ithaca College Library art books and Napoleonic sources, out of more than a hundred contemporary images of Napoleon, I can find only two other depictions of Napoleon in "characteristic pose." One was an engraving by L. Jehotte à Liège, for which I can't find a date, in a book written in a language I can't read *(Napoleon I: Empereur des français)*. The other was a caricature done by George Cruickshank in 1814. (John Ashton, *English Caricature and Satire on Napoleon I.*)

Both the David painting and the Cruickshank caricature are depictions of Napoleon as an aging figure. David does it as "a final homage" (Johnson, p. 216); Ashton describes the Cruickshank cartoon this way: "With one hand in the breast of his coat, and the other thrust deep into his breeches pocket, suffering, too, from the impertinent inquisitiveness of the natives, it is no wonder he appears downcast" (p. 387). The David painting went to Britain after it was completed, but whether or not Cruickshank was familiar with it by 1814, I can't tell.

John Henderson
Reference Librarian
Ithaca College Library
Ithaca, NY

 Well, I had a conversation concerning our Napoleon question this weekend with a faculty member from the art history department at Ithaca College, and he said, "Funny you should ask. That subject was discussed in the latest issue of *Art Bulletin*."

So, with *Art Bulletin* in lap (see Arline Miller, "Re-dressing Classical Statuary: The Eighteenth-Century 'Hand-in-Waistcoat' Portrait," *Art Bulletin* 77 [March 1995]:45–63), I can quote some significant passages. The article begins:

A portrait type that appeared with relentless frequency in England in the eighteenth century is the familiar image of a gentleman

poised with one hand inside his partially unbuttoned waistcoat. . . .
Of course, in real life the "hand-held-in" was a common stance for
men of breeding.

The article discusses English portraiture and caricature
primarily, but in the addendum Miller addresses the David
portrait of Napoleon:

Today the "hand-in" gesture is, of course, best known from its
personalized revival in the nineteenth century. Surely most people
would recognize the pose as Napoleon's inimitable trademark—
which David rendered indelible in his commanding portrait of
1812. Still, the gesture's meaning was as unstable as Napoleon's
reputation; *Pride* is the caption given to the attitude ten years later
in Henry Siddon's *Practical Illustrations of Rhetorical Gesture and
Action,* a text that was used as an acting manual. It is not surprising
that when Napoleon's reputation plummeted, a subtly arched
postural infliction made the gesture decidedly imperious.

Other portraits included in this article show the following
subjects with hand in waistcoat:

Horace Walpole, ca. 1734–35

George Frideric Handel, 1756

Samuel Richardson, 1750

Thomas Gainsborough (self-portrait), ca. 1759

Philippe de France, Duc d'Orleans, 1680s

Charles, 1st Viscount Townshend, ca. 1695

William Clayton, 1st Baron Sundon, 1719

John Henderson
Reference Librarian
Ithaca College Library
Ithaca, NY

◻ ◻ ◻

And If Four Hooves Are Off the Ground . . .

Q I have a patron who thinks he remembers reading that the placement of horses' hooves on a statue of a military person has a special meaning—one hoof raised means the person was wounded in battle, all hooves on the ground means the person died a natural death, etc. Does this ring a bell with anyone?

Carole Elmore
Reference Librarian
Newnan-Coweta Public Library
Newnan, GA

A Regarding the myth of feet placement on military statues, there is a lengthy discussion in "The Exchange," *RQ*, winter 1994, pp. 143–44.

I will quote just several sentences:

The number of the horse's feet taken up from the ground has nothing to do with any attribute of the person depicted and everything to do with the skill of the sculptor and his ability to overcome nearly insurmountable problems in solid geometry, stress of materials, and other aspects of civil engineering . . .

There is nothing but anecdotal evidence for this belief, and there are many exceptions to this supposed rule. For example, General Andrew Jackson's statue in Washington, D.C. has forefeet pawing the air, yet Jackson died at home. The New York City statue of General Sherman has two hooves in the air, but Sherman died years after the Civil War.

While the author who contributed this information to "The Exchange" (Frank Young) cites no authority for his conclusion, in the absence of any authority other than anecdotes (or pamphlets prepared by some Park Service), and given the extreme reasonableness of the various arguments advanced by Young, it seems like a reasonable answer to me.

Charles Anderson
Editor, "The Exchange," RQ
(Reference and User Services Quarterly,
a publication of the American Library Association)
Bellevue, WA

□ □ □

Amazing Art

Q A teacher for visually impaired students would like a list of famous artists who were visually impaired.

A James Thurber drew some of his marvelous cartoons when he was nearly blind. If you include writers and musicians as artists, then many more names come to mind. How about John Milton, who was blind when he wrote *Paradise Lost*?

Donald Barclay
New Mexico State University Library
Las Cruces, NM

A I know this is not the response you're looking for, but I'll post it anyway, since you didn't specify visual artists:

J. S. Bach (late in life)

G. F. Handel (late in life)

Francesco Landini (fourteenth-century composer, blinded in childhood by smallpox)

Ray Charles

Stevie Wonder

I'd be glad to name other famous composers and historical musicians with so-called disabilities, if you need them.

There are some more who are blind, but I can't think of them offhand. Beethoven's deafness, of course, is a classic example of a noninhibiting "disability."

Wasn't El Greco believed (by some) to have been astigmatic, and wasn't that belief cited to explain the distorted perspective in his paintings?

Nina Gilbert
Department of Music, School of the Arts
University of California, Irvine
Irvine, CA

 Here's what I find from ten minutes of noodling around on Nexis: there are lots of visually impaired artists and even more visually impaired writers and musicians. Very famous visually impaired artists include Monet, Toulouse Lautrec, Degas, El Greco, Mary Cassatt, Goya, and Van Gogh. Others, such as Georgia O'Keeffe and Piero della Francesca, became blind late in life. Two successful modern blind artists are Carolyn James and Michael Naranjo.

Fred R. Shapiro
Associate Librarian for Public Services
Yale Law School
New Haven, CT

Artists Who Went Insane

A patron wants "a list of artists who went insane, like Van Gogh." Painters are preferred, but others, even musicians, might do. All I've come up with are Edvard Munch (nervous breakdown) and maybe a Swiss artist Adolf Wolfli (*Books in Print* lists *Madness and Art,* about him).

A category of art called "outsider art" or "art brut" deals with art created by the mentally ill, but this doesn't seem to be what the patron's after.

Bill Thomas
Reference Librarian
County of Los Angeles Public Library
Lancaster, CA

 When I visited the Tate Gallery in London several years ago, some of the biographical information attached to the pictures indicated that J. M. W. Turner (English painter, 1775–1851) suffered from insanity, but the *Dictionary of National Biography* and *McGraw-Hill Encyclopedia of World Biography* just state that he became a recluse.

Scott Joplin (composer of *The Maple Leaf Rag*) was committed to the Manhattan State Hospital in 1916 due to mental deterioration from syphilis and died there in April 1917 (*Dictionary of American Negro Biography*, p. 371).

Denise Montgomery
Information Services Librarian
Odum Library
Valdosta State University
Valdosta, GA

 Some more for your list:

Gaetano Donizetti (1797–1848). Italian composer. Suffered from general paralysis of the insane and was confined to a sanatorium.

Henri de Toulouse-Lautrec (1864–1901). French painter. Admitted to an asylum in 1899.

Robert Schumann (1810–1856). German composer. Admitted to an asylum in 1853, where he died three years later.

Others I'm not too sure about:

Francisco José de Goya y Lucientes (1746–1828). Spanish painter. His work during the Spanish War of Independence contains themes of madness, torture, rape, and satanism.

Eugène Henri Paul Gauguin (1848–1903). French painter. Suffered from bizarre behavior, syphilis, and also attempted suicide. A friend of Van Gogh.

William Blake (1757–1827). English poet and artist. Suffered from hallucinations throughout his life.

If you can get hold of it, a good book to look through is Howells, John G., and Osborn, M. Livia, *A Reference Companion to the History of Abnormal Psychology*. It lists not only the disorders, but those in history who suffered from them.

Jo Orange
Librarian, Document Locating
National Library of New Zealand
Wellington, New Zealand

 I'm surprised that no one has mentioned Camille Claudel here. There was a movie in the last couple of years based on her life. She was a respected sculptor around the turn of the century in Paris, Rodin's assistant and mistress. She was institutionalized in 1913, where she remained until her death in 1943. A fascinating and frightening story.

Elizabeth Henderson
Reference Librarian
Lynchburg College
Lynchburg, VA

The Political Cat in the Hat

 Does anyone have information to confirm that Dr. Seuss was at one time a political cartoonist, especially between 1940 and 1950?

Terry Wirick
Information Services Librarian
Erie County Public Library
Erie, PA

According to *Current Biography,* 1968, "from 1940 to 1942 Geisel was political cartoonist for Ralph Ingersoll's controversial, anti-isolationist New York newspaper *PM,* and during the same period he did occasional propaganda drawings for the United States Treasury Department, the War Production Board, and the Committee on Inter-American Affairs."

Stephen Newton
New Castle, DE

 According to *Dr. Seuss* by Ruth K. MacDonald, p. 8, Geisel "was an editorial cartoonist for *PM* magazine from 1940 to 1942, his most notable contribution being his series of anti-Nazi cartoons ridiculing Hitler." The paragraph then goes on to describe his work with Frank Capra, including the "Why We Fight" series of films. And I thought he just did children's books!

David Lundquist
Shields Library
University of California, Davis
Davis, CA

Pope Joan

The patron is convinced "Pope Joan" existed, in spite of all the sources *(Catholic Encyclopedia, Reader's Encyclopedia, Encyclopedia of Catholicism)* that refer to Pope Joan as a myth or a medieval legend. Do any of you know of any sources that *do* assert that there really was a female pope way back in the early Middle Ages? The story was that "Joan" was disguised as a man and only revealed after becoming pope, perhaps by pregnancy.

Carolyn Caywood
Bayside Area Librarian
Virginia Beach, VA

There is a book by Rosemary and Darroll Pardoe, *The Female Pope: The Mystery of Pope Joan: The First Complete Documentation of the Facts Behind the Legend.*

The authors in their introduction say they undertook to write the book ". . . after becoming aware that the total acceptance of the female pope's reality in many feminist publications was based on no firm foundation. We hoped that with careful research we might provide that foundation, but at the same time we determined to be the first writers on the subject ever to set about the task without preconceived ideas, and to keep an open mind throughout. As agnostics with no strong feelings, either for or against the Catholic Church, neither of us had an ax to grind."

After examining the various sources and physical evidence both in Rome and elsewhere that is the body of the book, the authors in the afterword say, "Possible it may be, but as far as we can tell it never happened; unless of course she was one of the historical popes, and so perfect in her disguise that she went to her grave undiscovered. That is a wholly different question, and one which may never be answered conclusively."

Janet Irwin
Reference Librarian
Multnomah County Library
Portland, OR

 As much fun as we are having with this now (and may yet), the debunking of "Pope Joan" took place over three hundred years ago, and nothing since seems to have added any more clarity. Wendell Cochran has reminded me off-list of Gibbon's dismissal of the legend in volume III of the *Decline and Fall*. Even before that, the two most compelling works on the topic were David Blondel's *De Ionna Papissa* and Giuseppe Garampi's *De nummo argenteo Benedicti III (Regarding the Silver Coins of Benedict III)*. The two authors (one Protestant, one Catholic) cite documentation for the assumption of the papal throne by Benedict III within weeks of the death of Pope Leo IV on July 17, 855. The Emperor Lothaire died on September 28 of the same year, and Garampi—both cleric and archaeologist—unearthed coins and medallions dated 855 bearing the name of Lothaire as Emperor and Benedict as Pope. There was barely a two-month period when another Pope was possible. That seems more than ample proof that the alleged two-year reign of "Pope Joan" from 855 to 857 could not have happened.

As fascinating as the tale of the papissa is, the nefarious influence of the historical Marozia on the popes she manipulated about the same time is even more intriguing and scandalous. In fact, her misdeeds (and theirs) may have fed the legend of a female Pope for lo these many years.

John Dyson
Department of Spanish and Portuguese
Indiana University
Bloomington, IN

As I recall, your original question was not, "Was there in fact a Pope Joan?" but, "Can anyone name for me a source which claims that there was in fact a Pope Joan?"

A number of fellow wombats have offered good arguments for her nonexistence (and certainly I would agree), but that seems a bit beside the point of your original question (which noted that you had, in fact, found many works dismissing her existence).

One reference work that seems to shade its entry toward "wanting to believe," at least, is *The Woman's Encyclopedia of Myths and Secrets* by Barbara G. Walker, which showed up on Stumpers a week or two back in another context.

Its entry under "Joan, Pope" (pp. 475–478) includes such lines as "although her pontificate was better documented than many others" and "the official story now is . . ." and "but the real papess, if there was one, belonged to an earlier era than these—an era of untrustworthy, disconnected records, often destroyed by social upheavals and wars."

I would take the Pope Joan story with several more grains of salt than the *WEMS* does (several more salt shakers, in fact), but if you *are* in fact looking for a reasonably respectable recent reference work that seems as much pro as anti on the question, perhaps this will qualify.

Dennis Lien
Reference Librarian
Wilson Library
University of Minnesota
Minneapolis, MN

□ □ □

Crowded Pin

 What is the history of the quotation "How many angels can dance on the head of a pin?"

John Ronner, *Do You Have a Guardian Angel? And Other Questions About Angels,* pp. 30, 31.

HOW MANY ANGELS CAN DANCE ON THE POINT OF A PIN?

The top angel thinker of the Middle Ages, Thomas Aquinas, said angels are 100 percent pure spirits, having no matter or mass and taking up no space—like a thought.

So the answer is that every angel in God's cosmos could dance on the tiniest smidgen of a pinpoint and all of its space would be left over.

Most angel book writers assume that this question was one of many mind-game riddles of subtle logic by which medieval churchmen quibbled over angels' finer points in the Middle Ages.

However, the famed angel philosopher Mortimer Adler insists that the medievals never asked the question. In his book *The Angels and Us,* he says this angel cliche was cooked up by modern types to ridicule the intense speculations about angels during the Middle Ages (see "Angel Words—quodlibet").

p. 63:

Quodlibet: Subtle mind games in which angel scholars of the Middle Ages logically debated the very fine points of angels. The most famous of the quodlibets is "How many angels can dance on the point of a needle?"

p. 19:

When angels are mentioned, the question that usually pops into people's minds today is how many of them can stand on the head of a pin. That question was never propounded by any mediaeval theologian. It was an invention of modern scoffers who used it to exemplify what they regarded as the utterly specious disputes involved in angelology.

Unfortunately, Adler does not identify the "modern scoffers." Maybe Bishop Usher et al.? Incidentally, the front flap of Adler's book says "As for the question about the number of angels on the head of a pin, the answer is *only one*—for the same reason that there can be only one auto-mobile at a time in a parking space."

Bill Thomas
Reference Librarian
County of Los Angeles Public Library
Lancaster, CA

 Burton Stevenson's *Home Book of Quotations* (the best quotation dictionary ever compiled, by the way) has this:

Why, a spirit is such a little, little thing, that I have heard a man, who was a great scholar, say that he'll dance ye a hornpipe upon the point of a needle.
　　　Addison, *The Drummer.* Act i, sc. 1.

Some who are far from atheists, may make themselves merry with that conceit of thousands of spirits dancing at once upon a needle's point.
　　　Ralph Cudworth, *True Intellectual System of the Universe,* vol. iii, p. 497.

How many angels can dance on the point of a very fine needle without jostling each other?
　　　Isaac D'Israeli, *Curiosities of Literature: Quodlibets.* Paraphrasing an idea in St. Thomas Aquinas, *Summa.*

Fred R. Shapiro
Associate Librarian for Public Services
Yale Law School
New Haven, CT

□　□　□

The Saint and the Grasshoppers

 I have a patron who is looking for information about a Finnish St. Urho (or Uhro?). She believes that he has a feast day around March and has something to do with driving out grasshoppers. (A Finnish St. Patrick?) She would like to know anything about him—why famous, when (if) he lived. I checked everything we have that might have this. Hope someone can help.

Cindy McIntyre
Electronic Resources Coordinator
Romeo District Library
Romeo, MI

Ah yes, St. Urho, the patron saint of Finland. As legend has it, back in the days when legends were happening, the entire Finnish grape harvest, and hence the wine output, was threatened by a plague of grasshoppers.

Nothing is known of the parentage of the doughty Urho or his childhood. But he knew the call of duty, and with pitchfork in hand attacked the dastardly grasshoppers. The battle raged for three days and nights—since the sun was up continually it was hard to tell the difference—but at last the final grasshopper was banished from the soil of Finland.

After the grapes were picked and the crush was done, the grateful vintners canonized Rho by acclamation. Since then, the faithful celebrate the exploits of St. Urho every March 16th with the wearing of the purple (actually more a Pinot Noir color). The canonical symbol for St. Urho is a rampant pitchfork with impaled grasshopper sinister.

Don Stadius
InformAction
Portland, OR

A bit of midwestern, Garrison Keillor-ish type humor, rather than a real saint. I think his legend originated or is celebrated mostly around New York Mills, Minnesota (which has a lot of Finnish–American citizens). This is from memory.

Dennis Lien
Reference Librarian
Wilson Library
University of Minnesota
Minneapolis, MN

I forwarded the message to my Finnish e-mail pal, Tero Tommila, and apparently hit a major nerve! Here's what he says:

This is all total nonsense. There never existed any "St. Urho" in Finland or anywhere.

The fiction about some "Urho" is invented by the American Finns to compensate for the Irish feasting (particularly drinking, etc.?) of St. Patrick. So that the Finns in the U.S. had something to do (feast) during the springtime.

Nina Gilbert
Department of Music, School of the Arts
University of California, Irvine
Irvine, CA

13 People

A Rose by Another Name

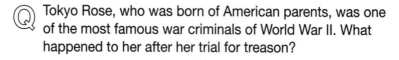 Tokyo Rose, who was born of American parents, was one of the most famous war criminals of World War II. What happened to her after her trial for treason?

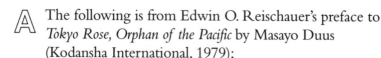 The following is from Edwin O. Reischauer's preface to *Tokyo Rose, Orphan of the Pacific* by Masayo Duus (Kodansha International, 1979);

> But there was certainly no single "Tokyo Rose," nor was any person ever discovered who had traitorously engaged in propaganda activities against the United States in the fashion attributed by some to "Tokyo Rose." The myth of "Tokyo Rose" settled on a helpless and hapless young Japanese American girl, Iva Toguri, who had been stranded by the war in Japan.

The author of the book claims Toguri was later vindicated. Other citations in our database are Rex B. Gunn, *They Called Her Tokyo Rose* and Russell Howe, *The Hunt for "Tokyo Rose."* I suspect some checking of magazine/newspaper indexes in postwar years, particularly much later, might turn up more information on Toguri.

Charles Anderson
Editor, "The Exchange," RQ
(Reference and User Services Quarterly,
a publication of the American Library Association)
Bellevue, WA

 Iva Toguri d'Aquino was tried for treason and sentenced to ten years, of which she served six. After her release she settled in the United States, successfully fought a deportation attempt, campaigned to clear her name, and was pardoned by President Ford on his last day in office in

January 1977. Sources: any of half a dozen standard one-volume handbooks on World War II, any of the three or four books written on her, *Facts on File,* etc.

Dennis Lien
Reference Librarian
Wilson Library
University of Minnesota
Minneapolis, MN

 From the *Chicago Tribune,* December 11, 1992:

History lesson: Among gifts Mike Singletary will receive Sunday in his final home game for the Bears is a genuine Japanese samurai warrior sword. It's an acknowledgement of Singletary's "Samurai" nickname. There's a neat footnote to the item. It was purchased from the J. Toguri Mercantile gift shop in Chicago, which is owned by Iva Toguri—otherwise known as "Tokyo Rose" in World War II. Still living, she received a Presidential pardon a few years ago.

Looks like you can give her a call.

Andrew H. Steinberg
Law Librarianship Student
University of Washington
Seattle, WA

Disabled But Famous

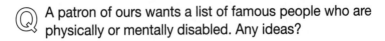 A patron of ours wants a list of famous people who are physically or mentally disabled. Any ideas?

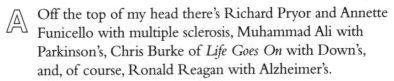 Off the top of my head there's Richard Pryor and Annette Funicello with multiple sclerosis, Muhammad Ali with Parkinson's, Chris Burke of *Life Goes On* with Down's, and, of course, Ronald Reagan with Alzheimer's.

Claudia Fitch
Louisville Free Public Library
Louisville, KY

Here are some from the music history corner. This information is available in standard biographies, and most of it can be found in *The New Grove Dictionary of Music and Musicians*. Not sure if these folks are the kind of "famous" you're looking for:

Beethoven was deaf. (I know, you knew that.) We don't really consider him "disabled," somehow.

Stevie Wonder is blind (you knew that too).

Bach and Handel were both blind by the end of their lives.

Scarlatti became too fat to play his harpsichord sonatas that called for hand-crossings.

Francesco Landini (medieval organist and composer) was blinded by smallpox as a child.

Robert Schumann crippled the index and middle fingers on his right hand, and was suicidal (institutionalized for "insanity").

William Billings (composer in eighteenth-century Boston; friend of Paul Revere) was described by a contemporary as "a singular man, of moderate size, short of one leg, with one eye, without an address, and with an uncommon negligence of person."

Hildegard von Bingen (medieval abbess and mystic; wrote plainchant and medical/herbal books) had visions that some have attributed to migraine. The popular Angel CD *Vision* features her chant; so do some other recent recordings.

Hermannus Contractus ("Blessed Herman the Cripple," 1013–1054) was crippled by a childhood disease. *New Grove* calls him a "Benedictine monk, chronicler, writer on scientific subjects (astronomy, arithmetic, music), clock- and musical instrument maker and composer."

Bedrich Smetana (Czech/Bohemian, 1824–1894) was deaf near the end of his life, and heard a high E inside his head. He wrote an autobiographical string quartet in E minor ("From My Life"), featuring a sustained high E.

I hope some of these are relevant. You may be able to find information in the Archives from the Stumpers search for visually impaired artists earlier this year.

Nina Gilbert
Department of Music, School of the Arts
University of California, Irvine
Irvine, CA

 Governor Gaston Caperton of West Virginia is dyslexic.

Thomas Jefferson suffered from migraines and from a broken wrist that never healed properly—both caused him considerable pain.

Both Abraham Lincoln and his wife had mental illness. Abe was said to be manic depressive, and Mary's grief after his death caused behavior so odd that her son had her put in a mental hospital.

Winston Churchill also suffered from "the black dog" of depression.

Lois Aleta Fundis
Reference Librarian
Mary H. Weir Public Library
Weirton, WV

 Someone suggested Bree Walker Lampley, the California anchorwoman with crippled hands and feet, for the question about famous disabled people. I found several articles about her using IAC's Magazine Index. She and her husband featured prominently in a controversy over whether those with genetic disabilities have the "right" to pass their condition on to children.

Lesley Williams
Electronic Resources Specialist
Arlington Heights Memorial Library
Evanston, IL

Jim Eisenreich of the Philadelphia Phillies has Tourette's syndrome.

Did anyone mention FDR?

And General George S. Patton, Jr., was dyslexic.

Sue Kamm
Associate Librarian
Inglewood Public Library
Inglewood, CA

 Luis de Camões lost his right eye fighting against the Moors in North Africa and went on to write the *Lusiads*.

Miguel de Cervantes wrote *Don Quijote* after losing the use of his left hand in the Battle of Lepanto against the Ottoman Turks.

Like John Milton, Argentine writer Jorge Luis Borges went blind in middle age. He has a nice poem, "El poema de los dones" ("Poem of the Gifts") on God's irony at having granted him the directorship of the Argentine National Library and blindness all in the same year (1955).

John Dyson
Department of Spanish and Portuguese
Indiana University
Bloomington, IN

 There is Jim Abbott, the baseball player with only one hand, and James Brady, President Reagan's press secretary, who was wounded in the assassination attempt in 1981, and who is now a motivational speaker (and the "Brady" in the Brady Bill gun control legislation . . .).

Donna Lowich
Research Librarian
Bellcore
Piscataway, NJ

I can think of at least two rock stars with hearing impairments: Pete Townshend of the Who and Brian Wilson of the Beach Boys. Pete's seems to be from standing too close to too many loud amplifiers (my dad, who is not famous, is hearing-impaired from working too close to too many loud trains) but Brian's goes back to some early childhood injury. Of course Brian has been most in the news for recovering from mental illness—some of which was the result of drug abuse, which leads to the question of whether drug/alcohol abuse/addiction counts as a "disability" in this regard. How about if the drugs cause actual physical health problems— liver disease (David Crosby; Mickey Mantle; Larry Hagman) or heart disease (Jerry Garcia)?

Lois Aleta Fundis
Reference Librarian
Mary H. Weir Public Library
Weirton, WV

 There was a report in the *New York Daily News* gossip column this morning that Sting is suffering from a degenerative hearing problem and may be losing his hearing. It has apparently been confirmed by his press people.

Barbara Bristow
Humanities Index
New York, NY

 Senator Dole's right hand was injured in World War II (while "leading an assault on a last-ditch German machine gun nest in the Po Valley of Italy on April 14, 1945," says the *Current Biography* [1987] article about him). "His right arm and hand were beyond recuperation, but his left hand had some residual feeling, and he finally mastered the use of that 'good' hand."

While that was happening there was Pete Gray, who played for the St. Louis Browns (now the Baltimore Orioles) in 1945 as an outfielder despite the fact that he only had one whole (left) arm—most of his right arm had been amputated when he was young (he "reached through spokes of farmer's truck for baseball just as driver put truck in motion"). In order to continue playing ball, he "developed skill in catching ball with gloved left hand, quickly slipping glove under right-arm stump, and throwing baseball to infield. At plate was able to anchor base of bat against body and hit ball, powered by strong left arm." He hit a respectable but not earth-shaking .218 in 77 games in his one major league season, including 6 doubles, 2 triples and 13 runs batted in (and 5 stolen bases!). In a doubleheader with the Yankees on May 20 he reached base 5 times (4 hits and 1 walk), drove in 2 runs, scored twice himself, and handled nine fielding plays ("chances"). (Quotes for this come from *Who's Who in Professional Baseball* by Gene Karst and Martin J. Jones, Jr.) Keith Carradine played Gray in a TV movie.

And I would be remiss if I did not mention Rocky Bleier, who played football at Notre Dame, got drafted twice—first by the Steelers and then by Uncle Sam—and was hit by shrapnel, severely injuring his feet and legs, in Vietnam. Doctors told him he might learn to walk again but would never play football, and the army declared him 40 percent disabled. Nonetheless, he returned to Pittsburgh and became part of the Steelers' Super Bowl teams of the 1970s as a running back.

Lois Aleta Fundis
Reference Librarian
Mary H. Weir Public Library
Weirton, WV

 Senator Daniel Inouye lost an arm as a member of the 442d in World War II.

David Lundquist
Shields Library
University of California, Davis
Davis, CA

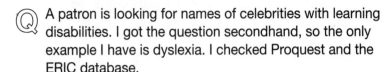

Learning-Disabled Celebrities

Q A patron is looking for names of celebrities with learning disabilities. I got the question secondhand, so the only example I have is dyslexia. I checked Proquest and the ERIC database.

Judy Hauser
Consultant
Oakland Schools, New Media Library
Waterford, MI

A One name that comes to mind immediately is the British actress Susan Hampshire, who has involved herself in information about dyslexia.

Even Flood
Reference Librarian
Norwegian DIANE Center
Technical University Library of Norway
Trondheim, Norway

A Science fiction author/critic/academic Samuel R. Delaney is dyslexic.

Dennis Lien
Reference Librarian
Wilson Library
University of Minnesota
Minneapolis, MN

A Try the various editions of the *Book of Lists* (Amy Wallace et al.), especially the new one, which includes a list of people with dyslexia. General George Patton and Nelson Rockefeller are two I remember off the top of my head.

Sue Kamm
Associate Librarian
Inglewood Public Library
Inglewood, CA

I'll contribute Stephen J. Cannell, who has created series such as *The A Team* and has just published his first novel as a dyslexic.

L. Jeanne Powers
Reference Librarian
Bristol Public Library
Bristol, VA/TN

Mega-Crowds

 We are trying to determine the "largest group of people gathered in the United States."

What we've found so far:

Million Man March—with estimates ranging from 400,000 to 837,000—and a New York Philharmonic concert in Central Park in July 1986 with 800,000 in attendance.

Any other ideas? or definitive answers?

Gretchen Raab
Reference/Adult Services Department Head
Neenah Public Library
Neenah, WI

 Earlier today someone asked what was the largest group of people to get together in the same place in the United States. According to the *New York Times Index,* 6 million people were on Manhattan Island on July 4, 1976. I don't know if this is a record, but it has to be close.

Stephen Newton
New Castle, DE

Vote Myth

Q Is it true that an early effort to make German the official language of the United States failed by only one vote in Congress?

A This is a fallacy. The question was not whether to make German the official language of the United States but a petition (in 1794) by a number of Germans residing in Augusta County, Virginia, to have "a certain proportion [i.e., a certain number of copies] of the laws of the United States . . . printed in the German language" as well as in English, and it was defeated not in an open vote but by the parliamentary maneuvering of a single man, the Speaker, F. A. C. Muhlenberg. For a full account of this "tradition," see Karl J. R. Arndt, "German as the Official Language of the United States of America?" in Karl J. R. Arndt and May E. Olson, *The German Language Press of the Americas / Die deutschsprachige Presse der Amerikas,* vol. 3, pp. 19–42.

Michael Palmer
Consultant Archivist
Claremont, CA

□ □ □

The Silent Majority

Q Laurie Anderson has a song with the lyrics:

Daddy, daddy, it's just like you said
Now that the living outnumber the dead.

Have we in fact reached the point when the population of the earth is greater than the number of people who have ever lived on the planet?

 I believe this riddle was posed in the *Mahabharata* and was supposedly asked by or to Alexander the Great when he was in the area. The answer to whether there are more men living or dead is living because the dead are no longer men. I know you want facts and figures, but I couldn't resist.

Charles E. Steele, Jr.
Science & Serials Librarian
Heterick Memorial Library
Ohio Northern University
Ada, OH

 The question of whether the living outnumber the dead often comes up in books that argue for or against reincarnation. (Are there enough humans alive today to recycle the souls of the dead, etc., etc.?) According to *Reincarnation: A Critical Examination* by Paul Edwards:

In an article published in the July–August 1981 issue of *BioScience*, Professor Arthur H. Westing of Amherst summarized the best available information about the number of human beings alive at various times. At the time at which he wrote, the population was estimated at 4.4 billion. In 1945 it had been 2.3 billion, in 1850 1 billion, in 1650 500 million, at the time of Christ 200 million, and in 8000 B.C.E. approximately 5 million. Among other interesting calculations Professor Westing estimated that the 1981 population of 4.4 billion amounted to 9 percent of all human beings who ever lived and that it was greater than the number of people who lived through the entire Paleolithic age, a period accounting for 86 percent of the duration of human life.

Since 4.4 billion is equal to 9 percent of all the humans who ever lived, the total number of humans who ever lived should be about 50 billion, give or take a few billion. In other words, the current population of the earth is currently dwarfed by the number of dead people who no longer walk the earth. Perhaps someone would like to look up the *BioScience* article to learn more about the source of Professor Westing's estimates.

Jon C. Pennington
Berkeley, CA

□ □ □

Skeleton in the Closet

Q Here's an intriguing question, and if you can answer it you'll save me a trip out to the local public library. We have nothing in our collection that can verify this story:

A reporter was told (by a scholar who should know, but didn't have a source) that when he was a young boy (age 12?) in Normal, Illinois, Adlai E. Stevenson was involved in a shooting incident (accidental?) in which a little girl was killed.

Can anyone verify this, with some reputable citation?

Kee Malesky
Reference Librarian
National Public Radio
Washington, DC

 The incident is recounted in John Bartlow Martin's *Adlai Stevenson of Illinois: The Life of Adlai Stevenson,* pp. 41–42.

In brief, it happened on December 30, 1912, when he was not quite thirteen years old. He was "hanging around" at a party given by his older sister Buffie, when one of the older guests offered to demonstrate the manual of arms that he had just learned. Adlai got a .22 rifle, and after the demonstration, the older boy returned it to him, presumably empty. The girl's name was Ruth Merwin, and while

most versions of the story say the gun went off accidentally while Adlai was putting it away, one eyewitness claims
that Adlai actually pointed the gun at her, though purely
by chance and not deliberately.

According to this account, the accident was never
mentioned except for two notes in Buffie's diary, and was
forgotten until 1952, when it was discovered by a *Time*
magazine reporter as Stevenson was being propelled
toward the presidential nomination. It probably appears in
a *Time* article at that time as well, but I don't have the
magazine here to check back that far.

Beth Bojack
Reference Librarian
Prairie View A&M University
Prairie View, TX

□ □ □

Slow But Deadly

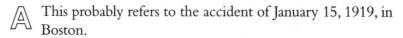

What are the details of a great molasses flood in Boston
that killed numerous people?

This probably refers to the accident of January 15, 1919, in
Boston.

A *Smithsonian* article in 1983 gives personal reminiscences
of the event, with photos. A storage tank 90 feet in diam-
eter and 50 feet tall (nearly full) ruptured at about 12:30
P.M. and 14,000 tons of molasses gushed into the down-
town area, forming a tidal wave 15 feet high and traveling
at speeds of up to 35 mph! It flattened buildings and
carried them away, knocked the props out from under the
elevated train, killed 21 people, and injured more than
150. Rescue workers waded in molasses muck up to their
knees, and spread the sticky stuff as far as Worcester when
they returned home. Supposedly the public facilities, such

as streetcar seats, in Boston remained sticky for months, and the high "water" marks on some stone buildings survived for years. The resulting litigation took six years, involving over 3,000 witnesses and so many attorneys that they couldn't all fit into the courtroom at the same time. The company that owned the tank was found guilty of negligence, and paid a total in settlement of between $500,000 and $1 million (a lot for those days). Families of victims received about $7,000 each. Presumably the rest went for property damages and/or lawyers' fees.

A similar incident with lesser damage occurred in 1989 in Nebraska. No loss of life, but serious property damage and a major cleanup effort resulted.

Gary Lee Phillips
Computer Services Librarian
Columbia College
Chicago, IL

 Here's the specific citation for the *Smithsonian* article:

Edwards Park, "Without warning, molasses in January surged over Boston." *Smithsonian.* November 1983, p. 213.

Michael A. Miranda
Benjamin F. Feinberg Library
SUNY, Plattsburgh
Plattsburgh, NY

Eco-Hoax

 On another list (ECOLOG-L), someone suggested that a well-known speech by Chief Seattle was a hoax. During the discussion it was claimed that a movie maker in the 1970's had made it up; then that claim was amended to an assertion that the movie maker significantly altered it. The last hoax claim was that Dr. Henry Smith, who published the speech in 1854, was not present at the occasion when both Governor (of the Washington Territory) Isaac Stevens and Chief Seattle (Seathl) met in Seattle and addressed settlers and members of the Suquamish and Duwamish tribes. Instead, the claim was made that in 1854 Smith stole a romantic, but fictional, speech from a German source to perpetuate the notion of a noble savage. The other list's contributors were not as good as Stumpers contributors usually are about documenting sources. So can anyone out there provide documentary evidence one way or the other as to the authenticity of Chief Seattle's speech?

We have two sources in the library that include the speech. Both accept it as authentic. The sources are W. C. Vanderwerth's *Indian Oratory* and Virginia Irving Armstrong's *I Have Spoken: American History Through the Voices of the Indians.*

John Henderson
Reference Librarian
Ithaca College Library
Ithaca, NY

 After dealing with this question several times over the course of years editing "The Exchange" in *RQ*, the most extensive documentation I've found comes from SCAN/INFO (Southern California Answering Network). Following are the comments in the summer 1993 issue of *RQ* (p. 463):

Professor Rudolph Kaiser, University of Hildesheim, Germany, identified four versions of the speech, and reports on them in *Recovering the Word: Essay on Native American Literature* (pp. 497–536).

1. Dr. Henry A. Smith's, published in the *Seattle Sunday Star,* October 29, 1887, and possibly written from notes he made thirty-three years earlier when he heard the speech on Main Street in Seattle.

2. William Arrowsmith's, published in 1969 in *Arion* (pp. 461–64) and the *American Poetry Review* (pp. 23–26, 1975).

3. Ted Perry's, who rewrote the Arrowsmith version in 1970–71 for a script for a film on pollution entitled *Home.* Perry says the speech is fictitious and that he probably shouldn't have used Chief Seattle's name. However, this is the version circulated most widely and tends to be the one asked for at reference desks.

4. A version exhibited in the U.S. Pavilion of the Spokane Expo 1974, based on Perry's version, but with an enlarged poetic style.

Charles Anderson
Editor, "The Exchange," RQ
(Reference and User Services Quarterly,
a publication of the American Library Association)
Bellevue, WA

 There was an article on this in *Newsweek,* May 4, 1992, p. 68. We have it clipped out and attached to a copy of the speech. Quoting in part from the article:

Chief Seattle did give a speech in 1854, but he never said "The earth is our mother." He never said "I have seen a thousand rotting buffaloes on the prairie, left by the white man who shot them from a passing train." The chief lived in the Pacific Northwest. He never saw a buffalo. . . . Those oh-so-quotable quotes were written by a screenwriter named Ted Perry for *Home,* a 1972 film about ecology. Perry wanted Native American testimony on environmental problems so he made up some eco-homilies and stuck them in Chief Seattle's mouth. Since then, the so-called Fifth Gospel speech has been widely quoted in books, on TV, from the pulpit.

We actually have two versions of the "speech," one of which is quite lengthy and includes the quotes mentioned above and a second one, credited with being translated by Dr. Henry Smith.

The second, from *The Eyes of Chief Seattle* by the Suquamish Museum, states at the bottom, after the quoted speech (which is quite short compared to the other one!):

There is much discussion about the accuracy of this translation. Many people believe that it was embellished with phrases that were not truly Seattle's. Nevertheless, the overall theme and the depth of its meaning are clearly reflected. Seeing, however briefly, the land we live in through the eyes of Chief Seattle, is a fitting tribute to this eloquent leader and the will of his people to survive.

Hope this sheds some light on the controversy. You might want to take a look at the *Newsweek* article in full for more info on the man who "invented" the quotes.

Deb Palmer
Reference Librarian
Cedar Rapids Public Library
Cedar Rapids, IA

☐ ☐ ☐

Last White House Slave

 Who was the last slave to serve in the White House?

 In his two-volume history of the White House, *The President's House,* William Seale gives some descriptions of each president's domestic arrangements. About Buchanan he writes:

He [Buchanan] then set out to restructure his household staff. Buchanan specified that the new employees were to be British, because he believed that people trained in the British system of domestic service would be less apt to threaten his privacy and peace of mind. They were accustomed to big houses, and loyalty was part of their ethic. The census of 1860 listed ten servants living under the Buchanan roof. Except for the butler, Pierre Vermereu, who was Belgian, they were from England, Ireland, and Wales. (p. 37)

Having ruled out Buchanan, I backtracked a bit, and found the following as the last mention of slaves used as servants in the White House, under the entry for Zachary Taylor:

Only four people in the Taylor White House could be characterized as servants, for the doorkeeper and the messenger were not, nor was the steward. Three housemaids and a butler, Charles Beale from Virginia, made a small number to serve such a large house. In his zeal to save money Taylor brought house slaves from Louisiana to supplement the four. There were approximately 15, including children; one was the body servant who had accompanied General Taylor to Mexico.

It seems clear that these slaves were restricted to the family's private rooms upstairs. They must have slept in the eight attic rooms. It was significant that Taylor hid his slaves from the public. By 1850 Northerners in Washington were increasingly uncomfortable about the presence of slaves.

For 20 years to come there would be very few Negro servants in the White House, and those would work in menial jobs or come only part time. Few ever held titles of important responsibilities. (p. 282)

Sorry not to have a definitive name for you, unless the body servant mentioned is named in a biography of Zachary Taylor. Hope this helps, anyway.

Beth Bojack
Reference Librarian
Prairie View A&M University
Prairie View, TX

□   □   □

The Long Version

Q We are trying to locate an example of the "full official title" of a British monarch/king/queen of times past, when the title took up half a page or more—found an excerpt in *Gloriana* by Luke on p. 44: "Queen of all England, France, Ireland, Defender of the True, Ancient and Catholic Faith, most worthy Empress from the Orcade Isles to the mountains Pyrenee . . . !," and footnote cites Strickland, *Lives of the Queens of England,* vol. 7, p. 156, which does not have that information at all! David Loades's *Mary Tudor: A Life* has Mary's will in Appendix 3, p. 370: "I, Marye by the Grace of God Quene of Englond, Spayne, France, both Sicelles, Jerusalem and Ireland, Defender of the Faythe, Archduchesse of Austriche, Duchesse of Burgundy, Millayne and Brabant, Countesse of Hapsburg, Flanders and Tyroll, and lawful wife to the most noble and virtuous Prince Philippe, by the same Grace of God Kynge of the said Realms and Domynions of Engand, &c."

Anything after the "&c."??? Have tried dozens of books, know I have seen an example of a full title before, but sure can't dig it up now that it is needed!

Jay R. Windisch
Reference Librarian
Timberland Regional Library Central Reference
Olympia, WA

 Mary's title is pretty unusual. Her official title stopped at ". . . Brabant." The following part ("Countess of Hapsburg . . ." etc.) was either unofficial, or the various parts were tacked on depending on the context of the moment. For example, William I was not simultaneously king of England and duke of Normandy. He was one or the other depending on the function he was performing. It was his great-nephew who fused the two titles. All the same, Mary probably had the longest title of any English monarch. Except for Mary, it is the twentieth-century monarchs who have had the longest titles. Lois Fundis also alluded to the English monarchs also being king or queen of France. That idea died hard; it was George III who finally dropped it.

Here are all the official monarchical titles since the Norman Conquest. The dates represent changes of title, not necessarily reigns. (Substitute "Regina" or "Queen" where appropriate.)

William I (1066–1087):
  Rex Anglorum.

William II, Henry I (1087–1135):
  Dei Gratia Rex Anglorum.

Stephen (1135–1154):
  Rex Anglorum Dux Normannorum.

Henry II, Richard I (1154–1199):
  Rex Angliae, Dux Normanniae et Aquitaniae et Comes Andegaviae.

John, Henry III (1199–ca. 1260):
  Rex Angliae, Dominus Hiberniae, Dux Normanniae, et Dux Aquitaniae.

Henry III through Edward III (ca. 1260–1339):
  Rex Angliae, Dominus Hiberniae et Dux Aquitaniae.

Edward III through Henry V (1339–1420):
  Rex Angliae et Franciae et Dominus Hiberniae.

Henry V (1420–1422):
  Rex Angliae, Haeres et Regens Franciae, et Dominus Hiberniae.

Henry VI through Henry VIII (1422–1521):
  Rex Angliae et Franciae et Dominus Hiberniae.

Henry VIII (1521–1542):
  King of England and France, Defender of the Faith, Lord of Ireland, and of the Church of England on Earth Supreme Head.

Henry VIII through Mary I (1541–1554):
  King of England, France and Ireland, Defender of the Faith, and of the Church of England and also of Ireland on Earth the Supreme Head.

Philip and Mary (1554–1558), theoretically reigning jointly:
  By the Grace of God, King and Queen of England and France, Naples, Jerusalem, and Ireland, Defenders of the Faith, Princes of Spain and Sicily, Archdukes of Austria, Dukes of Milan, Burgundy and Brabant.

Elizabeth I (1558–1603):
Queen of England, France and Ireland, Defender of the Faith.

James I through James II (1603–1688):
King of England, Scotland, France and Ireland, Defender of the Faith. [Note: Scotland was part of the title from the moment the king of Scotland became king of England, well before the formal political union in 1707, which changed the terminology to "Great Britain." Charles II legally commenced his reign upon the death of his father in 1649, but was in exile until 1660.]

William III and Mary II (1688–1702), reigning jointly:
King and Queen of England, Scotland, France and Ireland, Defenders of the Faith. [Mary died in 1694.]

Anne (1702–1707):
Queen of England, Scotland, France and Ireland, Defender of the Faith.

Anne (1707–1714):
Queen of Great Britain, France and Ireland, Defender of the Faith.

George I through George III (1714–1801):
King of Great Britain, France and Ireland, Duke of Brunswick-Luneburg, Elector of Hanover, Defender of the Faith.

George III through Victoria (1801–1877):
By the Grace of God, of the United Kingdom of Great Britain and Ireland King, Defender of the Faith, Elector of Hanover. [In 1814 "Elector" changed to "King of Hanover."]

Victoria (1877–1901):
By the Grace of God, of the United Kingdom of Great Britain and Ireland, Queen, Defender of the Faith, Empress of India.

Edward VII, George V (1901–1927):
By the Grace of God, of the United Kingdom of Great Britain and Ireland, and of the British Dominions beyond the Seas, King, Defender of the Faith, Emperor of India.

George V through Elizabeth II (1927–1952):
By the Grace of God, of Great Britain, Ireland and the British Dominions beyond the Seas, King, Defender of the Faith, Emperor of India. [George VI omitted "Emperor of India" by royal proclamation in June 1948.]

Elizabeth II (1953–present):

> By the Grace of God, of the United Kingdom of Great Britain, and Northern Ireland and of her other Realms and Territories Queen, Head of the Commonwealth, Defender of the Faith.

Different forms of the titles are used by each Commonwealth country of which the Queen is head of state. For example, in Canada her title is "By the Grace of God of the United Kingdom, Canada and Her Other Realms and Territories Queen, Head of the Commonwealth, Defender of the Faith," and in abbreviated form "Queen of Canada."

Charles wants to be "Defender of the Faiths." It is a well-intended gesture, but has infuriated the Church of England.

—Source: chiefly derived from *Debrett's Peerage.*

T. F. Mills
Serials Librarian
University of Denver Library
Denver, CO

□ □ □

Black Dutch Puzzle

Q Who are the Black Dutch? How did the name come into existence?

A This is for the Archives: I was told about this some time ago by a fellow wombat in what must have been a private message because it never turned up in my searches of the Archives when I needed the citation.

Anyway, the gist of it is that at this point there is no single definition of "Black Dutch," though the term is frequently used. To try to clear up the confusion, the National Genealogical Society announced in the December 1994

Quarterly that people who have "Black Dutch" in their ancestry are invited to send in what they believe the term to mean, any family history/stories to illustrate the meaning, and genealogical charts to show the lineage.

From the *Quarterly:*

One of the enduring mysteries of American genealogy is the ethnic identification of a group widely . . . referred to as the "Black Dutch." Legions of genealogists report traditions of descent from such ancestors—traditions often accompanied by strong convictions as to the meaning of the term. Yet these explanations conflict from one family to another, and even within individual families. Novelists and historians have treated the subject more vaguely, gingerly, or romantically. Anthropologists have recorded other traditions, as yet untested against solid genealogical evidence. (p. 297)

So at this point, the answer is that there isn't any one answer.

L. Jeanne Powers
Reference Librarian
Bristol Public Library
Bristol, VA/TN

15 Geography
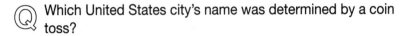

Probably Not Hoboken

Q Which United States city's name was determined by a coin toss?

A I did a cursory search on Nexis to find this, because I was certain the patron was looking for the wonderful city of St. Petersburg (hooray!), Florida, where yours truly works; and there is, indeed, a story about the naming of St. Pete that mentions the flip of a coin, resulting in a Mr. Demens winning the right to name the city, which he did, naming it after the Russian city.

However, the same Nexis search also brought up stories about coin tosses deciding the naming of Manhattan Beach, California (won by a New York native); and Portland, Oregon (another man, from the Northeast, wanted to name it Boston).

So, there you've got three candidates, from 1995 articles only, on Nexis—I have a feeling there may be more.

Sally G. Waters
Queen of Reference
Stetson College of Law Library
St. Petersburg, FL

A Portland, Oregon, was named (in 1845) by tossing a coin. Asa Lovejoy preferred Boston, but the toss was won by F. W. Pettygrove, who came from Maine. We old webfoots just know this, but it appears in print in *General History of Oregon,* by Charles H. Carey, p. 403.

Kathy Warner
Reference Librarian
Bellevue Regional Library
Bellevue, WA

□ □ □

Whence Cuba?

 Unbelievably, I cannot find the place-name definition of Cuba, the country. The only reference I found was to an American place-name that refers to "trough, tank" as the meaning. This was not what the patron wished to hear . . . the patron wanted to know the name's connection to a young princess. Could anyone assist me with a source for this?

Rhonda K. Kitchens
Tampa, FL

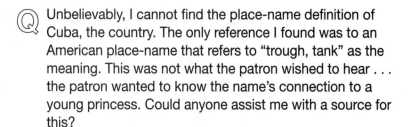 The *Enciclopedia Espase-Calpe* attributes *Cuba* to the contraction of an Arawak noun + adjective phrase *(coa bana)* meaning "big place." The problem is that *coa* in Arawak is neither a noun nor an adjective, but an adverbial particle meaning "still/yet/habitually." And *ba* and *na* are two particles that mean neither "big" nor "place." According to Sixto Perea y Alonso in *Filologia comparada de las lenguas y dialectos Arawak,* vol. I, pp. 60, 590, the noun *cuba* was then in use in the Guianas, where Arawak was still spoken. It meant "place of repose/[planted] garden/property." I think "place of repose" or "haven" must have been the original sense, and "garden/property" later meanings that accrued under European influence. There was also an Arawak verb formed from the same root that meant "to rest, to take one's ease."

Since *cuba* also means "keg/cask, [wooden] tub/vat" in Spanish, the name has given rise to lots of goofy etymologies, which is where "trough" and "tank" came from.

John Dyson
Department of Spanish and Portuguese
Indiana University
Bloomington, IN

Seven Seas

I'm sure someone here can give me an authoritative reference to the names of the original Seven Seas.

This is part of an ongoing project to collect groups of
sevens, from weekdays to dwarfs to Wonders of the World
to Pleiades . . . , so if you know of such a collection already
in existence, I'd love to hear about that as well.

Wolf Lahti
Allen, WA

1. The Pacific Ocean

2. The Atlantic Ocean

3. The Indian Ocean

4. The Arctic Ocean

5. The Mediterranean Sea

6. The North Sea

7. The Black seas, including the Baltic, the Aegean, and the
Arabian seas

—Source: John Boswell and Dan Starer, *Five Rings, Six
Crises, Seven Dwarfs, and 38 Ways to Win an Argument;
Numerical Lists You Never Knew or Once Knew and Forgot.*

Among the other related items included are articles of the
U.S. Constitution, stars in the Big Dipper, canonical hours,
Christ's last sayings on the cross, deadly sins, joys of Mary,
sorrows of Mary, holy sacraments, virtues, compartments
of hell, wonders of the ancient world, hills of Rome,
United Arab Emirates, warning signs of a stroke, types of
bone fractures, primary types of odors, warning signs of
cancer, Menorah, forbidden names of God, voyages of
Sinbad, ages of man, dwarfs, samurai, magnificent, against
Thebes, principles of man, principles of spiritualism, group

of, nations of the Warsaw pact, types of love, types of cats, Watergate, Chicago, colors of the spectrum, heptathlon, blocks of granite.

Chuck Cody
Reference Librarian
Columbus Metropolitan Library
Columbus, OH

□ □ □

Big Fall

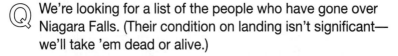 We're looking for a list of the people who have gone over Niagara Falls. (Their condition on landing isn't significant—we'll take 'em dead or alive.)

We've searched *Book of Lists* (1 and 2), *Guinness Book of World Records, People's Almanac, Guinness Book of Answers, New York Public Library Desk Reference, Reader's Guide Abstracts, PAPERS, World Almanac, Information Please Almanac, Periodical Abstracts,* Yahoo, AltaVista, HotBot, Article1st (FirstSearch), America: History & Life. I picked up a few names from that list, but nothing like a complete list (or even a partial listing).

Laura Watson
Reference Consultant
Shawnee Library System
Carterville, IL

 I don't know if this was previously overlooked, but the *Book of Lists #2* has the list "7 Persons Who Have Gone Over Niagara Falls in Barrels" on pp. 140–41. The text is not totally clear on this point, but it appears to be an exhaustive list of everyone who ever went over Niagara Falls in a barrel. The seven people are Annie Edson Taylor (1901); Bobby Leach (1911); Charles Stephens (1920); Jean Lussier (1928); George Stathakis (1930); William "Red" Hill, Jr. (1951); and William Fitzgerald (1961). Taylor, Leach, Lussier, and Fitzgerald survived; Stephens, Stathakis, and Hill all died. You can look to the *Book of Lists #2* to provide you with further information.

Jon C. Pennington
Berkeley, CA

 Here are a few "going over Niagara Falls" points from the *Journal's* database:

October 24, 1901—Annie Edison Taylor, a fifty-year-old widow, is the first person known to survive a trip over Niagara Falls in a barrel. She was strapped in her barrel with a leather harness and surrounded by cushions. Taylor performed the stunt to raise money.

August 4, 1951—Daredevil and veteran riverman William (Red) Hill, Jr., thirty-eight, dies in an attempt to ride Niagara Falls in a contraption built of inner tubes and netting. A crowd estimated at between 100,000 and 200,000 watched Hill go over the falls. Hill's body was found August 7.

July 9, 1960—Seven-year-old Rodger Woodward becomes the first person to survive an accidental plunge over Niagara Falls. The American boy was swept over the 49-metre Horseshoe Falls after a rowboat overturned. The accident leaves Woodward with minor injuries.

July 2, 1984—Karl Saucek, a thirty-seven-year-old stunt man from Hamilton, Ontario, survives a plunge over Niagara Falls in a lightweight metal and plastic barrel.

And in a very literal example of "going over the Falls," in 1859 French acrobat Charles Blondin crossed Niagara Falls on a tightrope. He was known to sometimes carry objects to make his stunts more dramatic (like stopping for a glass of wine in mid-trip), but as far as I know, never a barrel.

Patricia Beuerlein
Edmonton Journal Library
Edmonton, Alberta
Canada

16 Government and Law

Almost, But Not Quite . . .

Q We had two offbeat questions today that I had little or no luck with; this is one of them. A man said there was a story in the news about a couple (in Illinois, I believe he said) accused of having shot a police officer who were trying to use in their defense a constitutional amendment that was passed by Congress in 1811 but never ratified by the required three fourths of the states. The patron said the news item referred to another provision of the proposed amendment, the part he was really interested in finding, that would make it illegal for lawyers to hold public office. (Why am I not surprised it never passed?)

He was also wondering whether this proposed amendment had a time limit (as is common with newer proposed amendments, such as ERA), or whether there was a possibility that it was still kicking around the statehouses and might actually someday become law, as the recently passed one about congressional pay raises did two hundred years after James Madison proposed it.

Does anyone

(a) remember reading or hearing about this news item? I apparently missed it (even when you read three newspapers a day, it still happens).

(b) have any idea where to find information on an amendment that was proposed so long ago?

(c) know of a list of all, or even many, such proposed-but-never-ratified amendments?

Lois Aleta Fundis
Reference Librarian
Mary H. Weir Public Library
Weirton, WV

There's an excellent—and quite huge—volume of the *Constitution of the United States,* published by the Library of Congress; the latest edition we have is 1987.

In it, one specific section (pp. 51–53) gives the amendments that were proposed, but not ratified by the states. There are only five of them:

1. Proposed Articles I and II of the twelve proposed amendments which (ten of them) became the Bill of Rights; Article I addresses how many representatives there will be in Congress, and Article II addresses the compensation for senators and representatives.

2. In the second session of the eleventh Congress, an amendment was proposed to bar from citizenship any U.S. citizen who accepted a title of nobility from another government.

3. In 1861 an amendment was proposed to ban any amendments that would allow Congress to interfere with domestic institutions of any state.

4. In 1924 a child labor amendment was proposed.

5. And then there's the ERA, which formally died on June 30, 1982.

Also, according to the same section of the book, Congress has required ratification of an amendment within seven years of the time it is submitted to the states for ratification (this rule was introduced with the Eighteenth Amendment).

Sally G. Waters
Queen of Reference
Stetson College of Law Library
St. Petersburg, FL

 A sudden memory of junior high English class surfaces: Wasn't this one of the arguments Daniel Webster (the character, not the real politician) uses in Benet's play *The Devil and Daniel Webster*—that no American could serve a "foreign prince," in other words, the Devil? And the Devil proceeds to prove he isn't the least bit foreign to American history, but never challenges the premise.

Carolyn Caywood
Bayside Area Librarian
Virginia Beach, VA

 PART ONE This information is from the following article: Michael Pearson, "Death Row Couple Seeks to Topple Entire Judiciary," *Houston Chronicle,* September 1, 1996.

In 1811, Congress approved an amendment that would have outlawed public service by Americans who took knighthoods or other titles from foreign governments. An outgrowth of strong American patriotic sentiment as America was preparing for a second war with Great Britain, it was approved by Congress in 1811, but never ratified by the states. The death row inmates in question shot a police officer when he tried to flee after approaching their car and being fired upon. They claim the amendment was ratified in 1819 and prohibits lawyers and others with government licenses from serving in public office. As proof, they have produced several nineteenth-century copies of the Constitution that include the amendment. They say the amendment means lawyers, judges, prosecutors—even police officers—are all in office illegally. So they claim that neither the police officer they shot nor the judges who sentenced them have any constitutional power over them.

PART TWO In her query Lois enquired about other "proposed" constitutional amendments that were never passed, and I have seen various answers to this question;

however, there should be an important distinction made between amendments merely proposed and amendments passed by Congress.

Our Constitution is extraordinarily difficult to amend. Article V of the Constitution provides these methods. Basically, three steps must be taken to add an amendment to the Constitution:

Step 1: A congressional representative proposes an amendment.

Step 2: Congress approves the amendment. (Alternatively, the legislatures of two-thirds of the states may request that Congress call a constitutional convention, but of course, we have never had a second constitutional convention.)

Step 3: Amendments proposed by either route become valid only when ratified by three-fourths of the states.

—Source: Kathleen M. Sullivan, "Constitutional Constancy: Why Congress Should Cure Itself of Amendment Fever," 17 *Cardozo Law Review* 691 (1996).

Step 1 Congressional representatives have proposed thousands of constitutional amendments. The most recent number I found indicated over eleven thousand such amendments have been introduced in Congress. (See Sullivan article cited above.)

Step 2 For anything to result from these proposed amendments, both houses of Congress must approve them by a two-thirds vote. Of the more than eleven thousand amendments proposed, only thirty-three have been so approved.

Step 3 Three-fourths of the states must then ratify the proposed amendments. Of the thirty-three approved by Congress, twenty-seven have been ratified by the states. The deadline for ratification is seven years after passage by Congress (although a three-year extension was given in the case of the ERA). So there have been six constitutional amendments proposed by members of Congress and approved by two-thirds of both houses of Congress, but not ratified by the states.

Unfortunately, I have not found a single source that lists all six, so the list below is compiled from the article by Kathleen M. Sullivan cited above and the list Sally Waters from Stetson College of Law provided from a publication of the Library of Congress.

1. In 1978 a D.C. statehood proposal emerged from Congress but was never ratified by the states.

2. In 1972 Congress voted to send the ERA to the states for ratification with a seven-year deadline, but even with a three-year extension, the effort collapsed in 1982 three states short of the thirty-eight needed.

3. In 1924 an amendment banning child labor was never ratified.

4. In 1861 Congress approved an amendment to ban any amendments that would allow Congress to interfere with domestic institutions of any state.

5. In 1811, Congress approved an amendment to outlaw public service by Americans who took knighthoods or other titles from foreign governments.

6. In 1789, Article I of the twelve original amendments proposed by the first Congress addressed how many representatives there will be in Congress but was never ratified by the states. (The first Congress in 1789 proposed twelve amendments. Ten of them were passed and became the Bill of Rights. Articles I and II of the twelve proposed amendments were not so successful; however, Article II, which proposed barring congressional pay raises until after the subsequent election, was finally ratified and promulgated in 1992 to become the most recent amendment—the twenty-seventh. See article cited above.)

Rebecca Merritt Bichel
Lexington, VA

□   □   □

Black Helicopter Doings

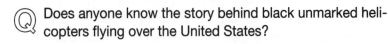

Q Does anyone know the story behind black unmarked helicopters flying over the United States?

A The question about black helicopters came up a while back. They were mentioned in an article, "Extremists Bracing for New World Order," in the *San Francisco Chronicle,* April 25, 1995.

According to the article, black helicopters figure prominently in the world of right-wing militias. They believe the black helicopters belong to the "Zionist Occupation Government" that runs the country in secret.

The article also says that the military and some federal agencies do fly black helicopters.

Donald A. Barclay
New Mexico State University Library
Las Cruces, NM

□ □ □

At Least They Wouldn't Admit to It . . .

Q I've seen several references to a remark reportedly made by Pauline Kael, former movie critic for the *New Yorker,* just after Richard Nixon's election to the presidency. She is supposed to have said, "I can't understand how he got elected; I don't know a single person who voted for him!"

Can anyone give me any details on when or where this remark was made and/or reported?

Mark Halpern
Senior Technical Editor
Scopus Technology
Emeryville, CA

Administration has only current information—no historical background. Any ideas?

Pam McLaughlin
Fremont Public Library
Mundelein, IL

 Apparently there is actually no way to tell who was issued the first card.

According to *A Brief History of Social Security: Social Security's 60th Anniversary* (document number 21059), the first Social Security card was issued to John Sweeney, Jr., of New Rochelle, New York, on December 1, 1936.

When this pamphlet first appeared, Ann Lewandowski, the public affairs specialist at our local Social Security office, received a letter from a person containing a photocopy of that individual's Social Security card, which was dated November 1936.

Ms. Lewandowski phoned the Social Security historian. He informed her that at the time the first Social Security cards were being distributed, thousands were being processed, resulting in some confusion. Mr. Sweeney was arbitrarily chosen as "first card recipient" for a ceremony on the aforementioned date. The lowest card number was that of Grace Dorsey Owen (001-01-0001), which I guess could give her a claim to the first card. However, since the numbers were distributed in blocks and issued by region, there is no assurance that the lowest number was the first issued.

Terry Stokke
Reference Librarian—Sociology Department
Minneapolis Public Library
Minneapolis, MN

□ □ □

Like Humpty Dumpty

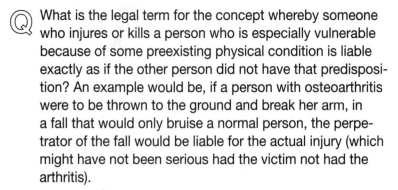

What is the legal term for the concept whereby someone who injures or kills a person who is especially vulnerable because of some preexisting physical condition is liable exactly as if the other person did not have that predisposition? An example would be, if a person with osteoarthritis were to be thrown to the ground and break her arm, in a fall that would only bruise a normal person, the perpetrator of the fall would be liable for the actual injury (which might have not been serious had the victim not had the arthritis).

Marian Drabkin
Librarian
Richmond Public Library
Richmond, CA

The legal term I think you're looking for is the "eggshell skull" theory; it's referred to this way in many, many cases.

Sally G. Waters
Queen of Reference
Stetson College of Law Library
St. Petersburg, FL

Other words are also used in enunciating the principle, though I don't know of any other name for it.

From *Tort Law* by R. W. M. Dias and B. S. Markesinis, after a mention of "injury to persons suffering from eggshell skulls or haemophilia . . .":

A defendant takes his victim *talem qualem,* i.e. as he finds him.

Criminal Law, 6th edition, by J. C. Smith and Brian Hogan quotes Lawton LJ in *R v. Blaue* (1975) 3 All ER 446, [1976] Crim LR 648:

It has long been the policy of the law that those who use violence on other people must take their victims as they find them.

These books are both about English law, of course.

John Rickard
Software Engineer
Cambridge, England

☐ ☐ ☐

Don't Xerox My Kleenex

 Is there a term describing words such as *cellophane* and *thermos* that were formerly trademarks but now have a generic meaning?

 We have had this question in the past, and according to Laurence Urdang at *Verbatim,* the process of a word going from brand name to generic is called *generification*; the word itself is called a *generic.* However, he said that *Band-aid, Kleenex, Xerox, Dixie Cup,* etc. are *not* generics, because their parent companies fight their use as generic terms. He gave two examples of words that *are* generics: *cellophane* and *thermos.* There are two articles about this in *Verbatim* magazine: "Word Law" by Dennis Baron (vol. 16, no. 1, summer 1989); and "Brand New Eponyms" by Richard Lederer (vol. 12, no. 1, summer 1985).

Thanks to Pat Guy at BALIS, which is where I got my file from.

Rosy Brewer
Reference Librarian
Monterey Bay Cooperative Library System (MOBAC)
Monterey, CA

Last night I was listening to "Net Talk" on a local station when they interviewed Herbert Lichtman of Markwatch, "a product that monitors the Internet for trademark and intellectual property infringements." Herbert works closely with trademarks and their owners and said *genericide* is the legal term for turning a trademark name into a generic word.

Tim Elliott
Co-ordinator, Information Services
AGRA Monenco Inc.
Calgary, Alberta
Canada

17 Crime and Punishment

Fateful Vehicle

Q What kind of automobile was Archduke Franz Ferdinand riding in when he was assassinated on June 28, 1914, in Sarajevo? What is the legend or history of what became of the car afterwards?

A Frank Edwards, *Stranger than Science,* pp. 163–66 (chap. 40, "The Cursed Car"), recounts a series of owners' accidents and misfortunes, concluding thus:

> It had killed 16 persons. It had helped to start one world war; and it remained for another war to destroy it—for the curse of the red car [Edwards describes it as a bright red six-passenger touring car and as a brand-new, bright red phaeton] was ended by an Allied bomb during World War II.

Yeah, right. Gretchen Goekjian, confirmed by Dennis Lien, recalled that the car wound up in the Museum of Military History in Vienna, Austria, where it is still on display.

Bill Thomas
Reference Librarian
County of Los Angeles Public Library
Lancaster, CA

A The 1991 *Cambridge Guide to Museums of the World,* p. 16, confirms the memory of Gretchen Goekjian that this automobile is in the Museum of Military History in Vienna, Austria, specifically:

> A separate room commemorates the immediate cause of the First World War, the assassination of the Archduke Ferdinand in

Sarajevo in June 1914. The exhibits include the uniform being worn by the Archduke and the motorcar in which the murder took place.

Contact information for this museum:

Heeresgeschichtliches Museum
Arsenal, Obj. 1
A-1030 Wien
Telephone: 0222 782303
Open Saturdays through Thursdays, 10–4 (minus major holidays)

Dennis Lien
Reference Librarian
Wilson Library
University of Minnesota
Minneapolis, MN

□   □   □

Female Assassination Victims

 We are trying to come up with a list of females who were assassinated. Have come up with Indira Gandhi and perhaps (?) Marilyn Monroe.

Attempted assassinations would also be included.

Ellen H. Ehrig
Associate Director for Information Services
Hinkle Library
SUNY College of Technology
Alfred, NY

 Don't forget Archduke Ferdinand's duchess, Sophie. I guess you might count the Romanov women, too, although that was more of an execution than an assassination.

Donald A. Barclay
New Mexico State University Library
Las Cruces, NM

What about Rosa Luxembourg, the Communist activist, assassinated by the Nazis in 1919?

Cora Ovens
Information Officer
UOFS Library and Information Services
Bloemfontein, South Africa

 I just stumbled on a source that may complement the Facts on File encyclopedia of assassinations that somebody mentioned:

Patrick Brogan, *The Fighting Never Stopped: A Comprehensive Guide to World Conflict Since 1945.*

Originally published in 1989 as *World Conflicts,* it includes an appendix chronologically listing assassinations since 1945. The only way to pick out the females is to read the whole list and hope you recognize women's names in different cultures. Here's my attempt:

1949 April 29 WIDOW of President Quezon of Philippines, and DAUGHTER.

1974 August 15 WIFE of President Park Chung Hee of South Korea (during failed attempt on his life; he was killed 26 October 1979).

1974 September 30 General Carlos Prats, former Chilean defense minister, and WIFE.

1976 July 21 Christopher Ewart-Biggs, U.K. ambassador to Dublin, and his SECRETARY, Judith Cook.

1976 September 21 Orlando Letelier, former Chilean foreign minister, and his SECRETARY Ronni Moffitt.

1977 April 10 Al-Qadi al-Hajri, former North Yemen prime minister, and his WIFE.

1980 August 15 Imam Sayyid Muhammed Baqir al-Sadr, Iraqi Shiite leader, and his SISTER.

1984 October 12 Attempt on Margaret Thatcher, British prime minister (four others killed).

1984 October 31 Indira Gandhi, prime minister of India.

1986 October 25 General Rafael Garricho Gil, governor of
Guipuzcoa, Spain, and his WIFE and son.

1987 April 25 Maurice Gibson, Northern Ireland appeals court
judge, and his WIFE.

If the list is reasonably comprehensive, only two of the
female victims were the assassin's principal target. It is sadly
significant that most of the others didn't even rate being
named in this list.

Footnote about the book for anybody considering it as a
valuable reference source: It is not as comprehensive as the
subtitle suggests. It includes only those conflicts still
flaming, simmering, or experiencing residual effects at the
time of writing. Some major wars, notably the Algerian
war of independence, the Congo civil war, the Greek civil
war, the Cuban revolution, the Biafran war, the Rhodesian
civil war, and British colonial conflicts such as with the
Kenyan Mau Mau, are all omitted.

T. F. Mills
Serials Librarian
University of Denver Library
Denver, CO

□ □ □

Monarchical Mortality

 Was Mary, Queen of Scots the first monarch to be
executed in Britain?

 Among my odd collections of odd objects is a collection
of loose papers that have fallen out of books returned to
libraries by borrowers, found in secondhand books I've
perused, etc. (Have not yet turned up one of the proverbial bacon strip bookmarks, alas.)

The following item, scissored from some unidentified
publication, is from this collection. Although, from the

context of the partial article printed on the back of it (a biographical sketch of a New York City business man, still living, who retired in 1872), I suspect that the publication may have been American, every time I look at this clipping, I seem to see and hear generations of English public school boys droning its listing in unison as they commit it to memory. Here are its contents:

The kings and queens of England since the Norman Conquest have died from the causes and at the ages herewith given:

Name	Age	Cause
William I	60	Rupture and fever
William II	43	Killed by an arrow
Henry I	67	Surfeit of lampreys
Stephen	49	The piles
Henry II	55	Grief
Richard I	43	Killed by an arrow
John	49	Poison
Henry III	65	Exhaustion of vital sources
Edward I	67	Diarrhoea
Edward II	43	Murdered
Edward III	65	Grief at death of his son
Richard II	33	Consumption
Henry IV	46	Apoplexy
Henry V	33	Pleurisy
Henry VI	49	Murdered
Edward IV	41	Ague
Edward V	12	Smothered
Richard III	42	Killed in battle
Henry VII	52	Consumption
Henry VIII	55	Ulcerated leg
Edward VI	15	Consumption
Mary	42	Small-pox
Elizabeth	69	Heart disease
James I	58	Ague
Charles I	48	Beheaded
Charles II	54	Apoplexy
James II	67	Dropped dead while praying
Mary II	32	Small-pox
William III	52	Fall from his horse
Anne	49	Apoplexy
George I	67	Paralytic attack

George II	77	Heart disease
George III	82	Insanity
George IV	68	Bursting of a blood vessel
William IV	72	Apoplexy

Martha Ann Mueller
(retired from) Scholes Library of Ceramics
NYS College of Ceramics
at Alfred University
Alfred, NY

□　□　□

Last Execution

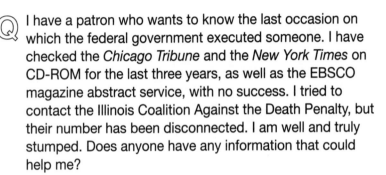

I have a patron who wants to know the last occasion on which the federal government executed someone. I have checked the *Chicago Tribune* and the *New York Times* on CD-ROM for the last three years, as well as the EBSCO magazine abstract service, with no success. I tried to contact the Illinois Coalition Against the Death Penalty, but their number has been disconnected. I am well and truly stumped. Does anyone have any information that could help me?

Pam McLaughlin
Fremont Public Library
Mundelein, IL

According to some articles found on Nexis, the last federal prisoner executed was Victor Feguer, executed in Iowa for murder and kidnapping, in 1963 (death by hanging); the last federal military prisoner executed was John Bennett, hanged in 1961 at Leavenworth, Kansas.

Most of the articles concerning this were from March 1995, when a federal prisoner, David Ronald Chandler, was scheduled to die after receiving a death sentence under the Anti-Drug Abuse Act of 1988. He was scheduled to receive a lethal injection at the federal prison in

Terre Haute on March 30, but apparently has now been given an indefinite stay of execution.

Sally G. Waters
Queen of Reference
Stetson College of Law Library
St. Petersburg, FL

□ □ □

Island Hideaways

 One of our clients is presenting a lecture about a local island that was once a prison. She wishes to demonstrate the historic use of islands in this way by listing some well-known people imprisoned or exiled on islands. Can anyone add to her brief list of Napoleon and Al Capone?

Kathy Buckley
Librarian-in-Charge
Queensland Museum
South Brisbane, Australia

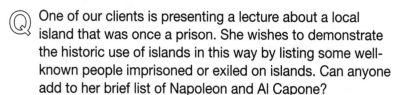 The Bounty crew on Pitcairn Island were certainly in exile.

Walt Howe
Delphi Forum Manager
Woburn, MA

 How about Papillon (Henri Charrière), Alfred Dreyfus, Nelson Mandela, Dr. Samuel Mudd, "Bird Man of Alcatraz" (Robert Stroud), and Fidel Castro?

Charrière and Stroud became famous in their roles as prisoners, so they may not meet the criteria.

Andrew Steinberg
Law Librarianship Student
University of Washington
Seattle, WA

Here are some more names.

Riker's Island

    Bernhard Goetz

    Al Sharpton (for fifteen days)

    William Marcy (Boss) Tweed

    Mae West (ten days for indecent performance)

    Robert Chambers

    Mark Chapman (temporarily)

North Brother Island

    Mary Mallon (Typhoid Mary)

Andrew H. Steinberg
Law Librarianship Student
University of Washington
Seattle, WA

 Dr. Samuel Mudd, who was found guilty of treating John Wilkes Booth's broken leg, was sentenced to life imprisonment at Fort Jefferson on the island of Dry Tortugas, which lies about sixty-eight miles southwest of Key West, Florida. (The place is now maintained as a national park; you can only get there by boat or plane.) When a yellow fever outbreak resulted in the death of all the army doctors there, Dr. Mudd volunteered his services and was pardoned as a result of this action by President Andrew Johnson. His health broken, he returned to his home in Maryland and died in 1883. (One of his relatives is newscaster Roger Mudd.)

—Source: Stewart Sifakis, *Who Was Who in the Civil War,* pp. 461–62.

Denise Montgomery
Information Services Librarian
Odum Library
Valdosta State University
Valdosta, GA

Torture Tales

 A patron has asked for the history of Chinese water torture. He wonders whether it was truly a Chinese practice, when it originated, and what else is known about it. He mentions that a couple of years ago he had this question submitted to the local, second-level reference service (BALIS at the time), but they couldn't find the answers.

Wendy Hyman
Reference Librarian
West Branch, Berkeley Public Library
Berkeley, CA

 This question was raised in the fall 1991 "The Exchange" *(RQ),* p. 11.

At that time SCAN (the Southern California Answering Network) did some extensive research. Staff contacted the editors of the *Oxford English Dictionary* and searched many word and language sources, including online databases, histories of torture, books on Harry Houdini (who developed the magic trick called "The Chinese Water Torture Cell") and books on the history of the Korean War. Even the evil Dr. Fu Manchu was mentioned. No source specifically identified the practice as Chinese in origin. The torture seems to be very old and used by many cultures. A later writer *(RQ,* spring 1992, p. 313), while lacking a specific source, remembered reading in some encyclopedia that the practice started in the Middle Ages.

Charles Anderson
Editor, "The Exchange," RQ
(Reference and User Services Quarterly,
a publication of the American Library Association)
Bellevue, WA

 One version practiced in the West was squassation: A thin cloth was placed over the face of the supine restrained victim. A trickle of water was directed straight down on the face. The cloth clung to nostrils and lips and conducted water into them. The victim couldn't blow or shake the cloth off because it clung. Usually they became distressed in a short time.

—From John Swain, *History of Torture* (one of my [insane cackle] favorite books!!).

O. H. McKagen
Blacksburg, VA

□ □ □

Unusual Furniture

Q Who is/was the murderer who made furniture from the bones of his victims, and was a biography of him ever written?

Dawn Marie Simpson
Marketing Coordinator
Westinghouse Power Generation Business Unit
Orlando, FL

A I believe it was Ed Gein (he also used skin for furniture!), and yes, there is a biography of him. Try *Deviant: The Shocking True Story of Ed Gein, the Original Psycho,* by Harold Schechter. This guy lived in a small town called Plainfield, Wisconsin, and after being caught, was sent to the psychiatric ward of Mendota Mental Health Institute in Madison, Wisconsin, where he died on July 26, 1984, of respiratory failure (p. 269). Fascinating stuff! This guy was a real sicko, and I believe he was the guy on whom *Psycho* was based.

I highly recommend the book.

Roberta Lincoln
Reference Librarian
Rockford Public Library
Rockford, IL

In many books about Gein—as well as books about the making of *Psycho*—it's pointed out that Robert Bloch was living in Wisconsin or thereabouts around the time Ed was arrested, and became interested in his story, using the basic premise (man lives in a house where he and his mother lived, shuts off her part of the house, kills women—and was totally dominated by his mother when she was alive) as the plot of his book *Psycho*.

The character of Leatherface in *Texas Chainsaw Massacre* was based on Ed (who wore the faces of his victims, both those he killed and those he stole from graves), as were the character of Buffalo Bill in *Silence of the Lambs* and an entire horror movie starring Roberts Blossom as the Gein-type killer.

The book by Harold Schechter is a wonderful piece of true-crime writing, in which he details the surroundings in Wisconsin where Ed lived and shows how he managed to go undetected for so long. There are at least two other books out, but they're much more lurid, poorly researched, and have as their only real selling point more pictures of Ed and his crimes.

Sally G. Waters
Queen of Reference
Stetson College of Law Library
St. Petersburg, FL

 The "horror movie starring Roberts Blossom as the Gein-type killer" is *Deranged* (1974).

Bill Thomas
Reference Librarian
County of Los Angeles Public Library
Lancaster, CA

☐ ☐ ☐

Unusual Wedding

 Serial killer Ted Bundy was engaged to Carol Boone prior to his execution. Did the marriage ever take place?

Dawn Marie Simpson
Marketing Coordinator
Westinghouse Power Generation Business Unit
Orlando, FL

 James Ellroy's book, *Murder and Mayhem* says:

Carol Ann Boone, one of many who believed Bundy, married him while he was on death row. To the embarrassment of Florida prison officials, she conceived a child with him during one of her routine visits. (p. 32)

Patricia Guy
University Place, WA

 Was Ted Bundy a notary? The reason we ask is because he supposedly joined himself and C. Boone together in matrimony while he was cross-examining her on the witness stand during one of his trials. Surely a notary can't conduct his or her own marriage ceremony?

Dawn Marie Simpson
Marketing Coordinator
Westinghouse Power Generation Business Unit
Orlando, FL

 I cannot answer the question about Ted Bundy being a notary, but I saw an *A&E Biography* about Bundy. The marriage exchange (for lack of a better term) occurred during his second trial, which was for the murder of a twelve-year-old girl, his last victim. The show contained the videotape of the exchange during the trial, and went something like this:

BUNDY: "Would you marry him?"

BOONE: "Yes, I would."

BUNDY: "I accept your offer of marriage."

This is from memory, and is not verbatim. However, I remember reading about this incident, and the author said that it was over and done with before the judge or anyone else had time to react. Nothing was said about Bundy being a notary, nor was the legality questioned.

According to *Biography,* Boone had a little girl by Bundy, after he was convicted and sent to prison. I guess Florida recognized the marriage as valid.

It sounds like a typical marriage under common law. I am from Texas, and my understanding of common-law marriage is that it requires only a public pronouncement, not an actual wedding. That pronouncement can be something as simple as saying to your friends in a bar: "Well, I've got to go home now. My better half is waiting for me." That, plus the knowledge of your friends that you are living with someone, is enough. The key is "public pronouncement."

Jeff Mullowney
Technical Writer
Richardson, TX

□ □ □

Teardrop Tattoos

Q Our morning was "brightened" this A.M. with the presence of a pro se patron looking for information about having his criminal record expunged. He had a teardrop tattooed just down from the corner of his eye, on his cheek. One librarian here believes that such a tattoo means that the person has served time for murder.

Any wombats there with knowledge of tattoo symbolism or such, who can confirm or give more info on such?

Sally G. Waters
Queen of Reference
Stetson College of Law Library
St. Petersburg, FL

According to *Street Signs: An Identification Guide of Symbols of Crime and Violence* by Mark Dunston, teardrop tattoos "represent time spent in prison. They have also shown up in other forms of criminal identification and represent murders committed by the wearer. Teardrops have also been reported to represent the death of gang members."

Of course, people could tattoo teardrops on their face for any reason, so you can't really know for sure!

Christine A. Whittington
Head of Reference and Assistant Access Services Librarian
Raymond H. Fogler Library
University of Maine
Orono, ME

18 Military

Pigeon Projectiles

Q One of our patrons has heard that, in the days before radar, pigeons were trained to guide missiles to their target by pecking at cross hairs. He would like more information about these pigeon missiles.

A The patron is referring to an idea that B. F. Skinner had about fifty years ago or so. Prototypes of the mechanisms were built, and it was demonstrated that pigeons could perform the task; but to my knowledge, the military brass never liked it and did not recommend further work on the project. Yes, the pigeons were trained via operant conditioning to peck a disk that served as the guidance system.

David E. Johnson
Department of Psychology
John Brown University
Siloam Springs, AR

A B. F. Skinner (1972), "Pigeons in a Pelican." In B. F. Skinner, *Cumulative Record,* 3rd edition, pp. 574–591.

The article is a reprint of a 1960 *American Psychologist* article. It outlines how this project, to put pigeons in the nose of a "missile" as a living guidance system, began in 1940 and continued off and on for another three to four years. In addition to Skinner, another luminary in the psychology of learning, W. K. Estes, also worked on parts of the project. The two were joined by a husband-and-wife team of graduate students, Keller and Marion Breland, who gained some notoriety in the 1950s as animal trainers for commercial purposes but also continued to do a significant amount of animal behavior research for the Department of Defense.

The original experiments didn't make much of an impression, but shortly after the United States entered World War II, the project was resurrected.

Pigeons were trained via operant conditioning to peck at a target on a disk. Their pecking was intended to manipulate the control surfaces of the "missile," which the researchers eventually found out was a gliderlike vehicle called a pelican (they had not been given much prior information due to security restrictions).

To make a long story even longer, the pigeons performed very well, but the project was dropped. Skinner, lamenting this rejection, wrote, " . . . we were offering a homing device, unusually resistant to jamming, capable of reacting to a wide variety of target patterns, requiring no materials in short supply, and so simple to build that production could be started in 30 days."

Sorry for the length of this post. That's what happens when you let an old professor on a soapbox!

David E. Johnson
Department of Psychology
John Brown University
Siloam Springs, AR

In Quest of Kilroy

 Where does the expression "Kilroy was here" come from?

 From *The Facts on File Encyclopedia of Word and Phrase Origins,* pp. 300–301:

It was first presumed that Kilroy was fictional; one graffiti expert even insisted that *Kilroy* represented an Oedipal fantasy, combining "kill" with "roi" (the French word for "king"). But word sleuths found that James J. Kilroy, a politician and an inspector in a

Quincy, Massachusetts shipyard, coined the slogan. Kilroy chalked the words on ships and crates of equipment to indicate that he had inspected them. From Quincy the phrase traveled on ships and crates all over the world, copied by GI's wherever it went, and Kilroy, who died in Boston in 1962 at the age of sixty, became the most widely "published" man since Shakespeare.

Beth Bojack
Reference Librarian
John B. Coleman Library
Prairie View A&M University
Prairie View, TX

 This story probably bears as much relation to the truth as most other colorful, undocumented etymological folklore, i.e., very little. Clyde H. Ward published an article on *Kilroy,* based on exceptionally diligent research, in *Psychoanalytic Quarterly* 31 (1962): 80. See this article, also the book *Motivations in Play, Games and Sports* by Ralph Slovenko and James A. Knight (1967), also the *Oxford English Dictionary,* for information about the word's history. The earliest documented usage yielded by these sources is *Kearns Air Force Post Review,* June 26, 1945, p. 5: "To the Unknown Soldier—Kilroy *Sleeps* Here." There is evidence that the expression was coined at this air force base. The second known usage is *Stars and Stripes, Pacific Edition,* August 19, 1945, p. 1: "Who the Hell Is Kilroy?" [title of article].

Fred R. Shapiro
Associate Librarian for Public Services
Yale Law School
New Haven, CT

The D in D-Day

 I've checked our dictionaries of World War II, abbreviation dictionaries, and descriptions of World War II. Can anyone tell me what the *D* in D-Day stands for? I've found that D-Day is used for the start of any military operation,

Normandy was just a "big" one. Is it for *due, detonation,* or something else?

Susan Hansen
Librarian
Rochester Public Library
Rochester, MN

 On Saturday our local PBS station (KXJZ, Sacramento) aired a discussion of just this question. The narrator/commentator stated that as a result of an enquiry he made to the Department of the Army Historical Research Branch, he learned that the meaning of the *D* in D–Day was "day" and that the meaning of *H* in H–Hour was "hour" and that, yes, it did mean that it was a redundant designation meaning Day–Day and Hour–Hour. He further went on to state that in France it is known as "J–Jour." He indicated that he expected to receive flak to the effect that it had other, more specific meanings but that, indeed, according to the military, the true meaning was as indicated above.

David Lundquist
Shields Library
University of California, Davis
Davis, CA

 From today's *New York Times* (June 6, 1994, national edition, p. A4):

> . . . D–Day originally meant nothing more than the day on which an envisioned military operation would be started. Phrases using repetitive initials go back at least as far as World War I and may have first been used in a September 7, 1918, field order of the Allied Expeditionary Force involving the campaign at the St. Mihiel salient in France. "The First Army will attack at H–Hour on D–Day," the order read. Because the Normandy invasion was such a momentous operation—the day of all days, so to speak—the phrase D–Day became associated with it.

Susan Krauss
Krauss Research
Oakland, CA

□ □ □

Ah, Bureaucracy . . .

 We're trying to locate the text of a humorous letter written by a naval officer whose requisition for toilet paper has been rejected. In the letter he explains, in deadpan military fashion, the function and necessity for TP. The letter was supposedly written by an officer during World War II; it might have been related to a submarine rather than a surface ship. I'm sure I've seen this myself at some point, but can't remember where, or even whether or not the account was fictional. I've performed a search of newspaper databases using Dialindex, but the story is apparently too old. Any takers?

Glenn Kersten
Research Librarian
Suburban Library System Reference Service
Oak Park, IL

 Thanks to all of you who helped to identify the story of a rejected requisition for toilet paper. Many had seen the incident in the movie *Operation Petticoat,* starring Cary Grant and Tony Curtis. Thanks to a tip from our patron, who had been visiting the Arizona National Memorial in Pearl Harbor, I managed to obtain a copy of the actual letter on which the movie incident was apparently based. The USS *Sculpin,* a diesel submarine damaged in the attack on Pearl Harbor, owns the original letter sent by the captain of USS *Skipjack* to the supply officer at Mare Island Naval Base in San Diego, in response to a rejection of a requisition for 150 rolls of toilet paper. The letter includes, nearly verbatim, some of the lines read aloud in the film, and carries a funny implication that the crew was helping to reduce nonessential paperwork by using substitutes for the missing TP.

Glenn Kersten
Research Librarian
Suburban Library System Reference Service
Oak Park, IL

Below is the full text (with a few minor errors possible, due to poor legibility of the original fax) of the response from the skipper of the USS *Skipjack* to a rejected requisition for toilet paper. As stated before, I obtained this from the archivist of Bowfin Park in Pearl Harbor, Hawaii. Many of you have pointed out that this real-life incident was apparently the basis for a scene in the movie *Operation Petticoat,* starring Cary Grant and Tony Curtis.

USS SKIPJACK

SS184/LS/SS36-1   June 11, 1942

From: Commanding Officer
To: Supply Officer, Navy Yard, Mare Island, California

Via: Commander Submarines, Southwest Pacific

Subj: Toilet Paper

Ref: (a) (4608) USS Holland (5148) USS SKIPJACK req 70-42 of
     30 July 1941
     (b) SO WYMI cancelled invoice No. 272836

Encl: (1) Copy of cancelled invoice
      (2) Sample of material requested

1. This vessel submitted a requisition for 150 rolls of toilet paper on July 30, 1941, to U.S.S. HOLLAND. The material was ordered by HOLLAND from the Supply Officer, Navy Yard, Mare Island, for delivery to USS SKIPJACK.

2. The Supply Officer, Navy Yard, Mare Island, on November 26, 1941, cancelled Mare Island Invoice No. 272836 with the stamped notation "Cancelled—cannot identify." This cancelled invoice was received by SKIPJACK on June 19, 1942.

3. During the 11-3/4 months elapsing from the time of ordering the toilet paper and the present date, the SKIPJACK personnel, despite their best efforts to await delivery of subject material, have been unable to wait on numerous occasions, and the situation is now quite acute, especially during depth charge attack by the "back-stabbers."

4. Enclosure (2) is a sample of the desired materials provided for the information of the Supply Officer, Navy Yard, Mare Island. The Commanding Officer, USS SKIPJACK, cannot help but wonder what is being used in Mare Island in place of this unidentifiable material, once well known to this command.

5. SKIPJACK personnel during this period have become accustomed to the use of "crests," i.e., the vast amount of incoming non-essential paper work, and in so doing feel that the wish of the Bureau of Ships for reduction of paper work is being complied with, thus effectively killing two birds with one stone.

6. It is believed by this command that the stamped notation "cannot identify" was possible error, and that this is simply a case of shortage of strategic war material, the SKIPJACK probably being low on the priority list.

7. In order to cooperate in our war effort at a small local sacrifice, the SKIPJACK desires no further action to be taken until the end of the current war, which has created a situation aptly described as "War is hell."

J. W. Coe

Glenn Kersten
Research Librarian
Suburban Library System Reference Service
Oak Park, IL

□　□　□

The American-Spanish War

Q I have found some sources for my patron, but if anyone can suggest the following, that would be great: My patron wants material on the Spanish-American War, but from the Spanish point of view. The patron does not read Spanish. Do Spaniards call the war by a different name (for example, the French and Indian War is called the Seven Years War in Europe)?

Mike Charton
Parsippany Public Library
Parsippany, NJ

Your patron's question prompts another question: which Spanish point of view? Just as there are differing American interpretations of the war, so there are Spanish. While the American jingoist perspective prevailed in 1898, later historians have opined that it was a dirty bit of imperialism.

I haven't checked to see if it has been translated, but Rafael Perez Delgado's *1898, el ano del desastre* (1976) discusses historiographical problems of the war. It is worth remembering that for Spain the war marked the definitive end of empire (for good or bad, depending on your perspective), and that Cuba, Puerto Rico, and the Philippines regarded it as wars of independence. A Cuban view of the prewar failure of diplomacy translated into English is Orestes Ferrara's *The Last Spanish War* (1937).

The year 1898 was a watershed in Spanish history, and it is often referred to as *"la generacion del 98"* and *"el noventa y ocho."* History books refer to the war as the "war of 1898" or the "war with the United States."

T. F. Mills
Serials Librarian
University of Denver Library
Denver, CO

It is unfortunate that your patron does not read Spanish, because T. F. is dead right: Perez Delgado's *1898* is a great book, and so is his *Maura*. The Spanish called the war *"la guerra contra los Estados Unidos,"* then *"el Desastre"* (the Disaster), because of its outcome, and later *"la guerra del 98."* Spanish newspapers and magazines in April and May 1898 are full of both jingoist and cooler heads, but the twelve-year-old king's military advisers prevailed, and the combination of monarchist machoism and U.S. provocation, plus Spain's harsh policies toward her few remaining colonies, led to the war.

The defeat led to a reassessment of Spain's place in the world (T. F.'s "watershed"), the chief spokesman for which was José Martinez Ruiz, better known by his pen-name Azorin. He and many others dragged Spain kicking and screaming into the twentieth century, along with philosopher José Ortega y Gasset, whose influential magazine *Revista de occidente* (Western Review) was a pointed effort at placing the country in the Western tradition they felt it had ignored for so many years. Both Azorin and Ortega published widely in the Spanish-speaking world in the most influential newspapers of the day to get their message out. Your patron might take a look at Donald L. Shaw's *The Generation of 1898 in Spain* (1975), at least to get a sense of what the Disaster wrought in a broad cultural way.

John Dyson
Department of Spanish and Portuguese
Indiana University
Bloomington, IN

□ □ □

At the Head of the Troops

Q When was the last time a European monarch actually led his own troops into battle, as opposed to sitting back in the palace and letting the cannon fodder take his whacks for him?

Pam McLaughlin
Fremont Public Library
Mundelein, IL

A Although war itself may be an atrocious and ridiculous pastime, it is quite appropriate and logical for leaders to let the cannon fodder take the whacks. The distinction between being in charge on the battlefield and actually using a weapon offensively or defensively may be too fine and insignificant to pinpoint effectively.

The battle of Dettingen in 1743 was the last time a British king (George II) commanded his army in person on the battlefield.

Napoleon III was both France's last monarch and the last one to command on the battlefield. After a string of defeats, he relinquished command to his generals in August 1870, but a month later was still on the battlefield at Sedan, where he was captured. His only son was killed on the battlefield in the 1879 Zulu War.

King Albert of the Belgians was personally in command when his army fell back on Antwerp during the German invasion of 1914. He remained in command throughout the war, and headed the final offensive in 1918. I don't know for sure, but I suspect Albert is the best candidate for the simplest answer to your question.

Christian X of Denmark, while not exactly enduring battlefield conditions, defied German authority and became a symbol of national resistance to Nazi occupation at considerable personal risk. The Germans placed him under house arrest in 1943.

In 1981 King Juan Carlos of Spain, nominally commander in chief, personally intervened to crush a military coup which naively expected his support. In the sense that he called on his loyal troops to assure the survival of democracy, he was leading in battle.

Perhaps the monarchy most closely involved with its military today is Jordan. Both King Hussein and his son went through rigorous officer training school in England (Sandhurst) and are combat pilots. The king was in command during the wars of 1967 and 1970, but probably not in quite the same strategic and tactical sense as Albert of the Belgians. Hussein has, through personal resourcefulness, survived dozens of assassination attempts.

In Britain, members of the royal family are still expected to fulfill their whole obligation should they be caught up in a war while performing military service. Prince Andrew served as a combat helicopter pilot in the Falklands War. His grandfather George VI may have stayed in his palace during the Battle of Britain, but that was the worst place to be for personal safety and the best way to show solidarity with his people's suffering. Although he walked around London's blitzed streets in the uniform of a field marshal, he was not in actual command.

T. F. Mills
Serials Librarian
University of Denver Library
Denver, CO

□ □ □

Tie a Yellow Ribbon

 Why is a yellow ribbon used to welcome soldiers back after a war?

 In the late 1970s Tony Orlando and Dawn recorded a hit song called "Tie a Yellow Ribbon" about a prisoner returning home, who wrote his girlfriend saying, "If you still want me . . . tie a yellow ribbon round the old oak tree."

When the hostages at the U.S. Embassy in Teheran were finally released in 1981, they were greeted with yellow ribbons tied on everything. After that they became a customary welcome for returning members of the military.

Charles King
Reference Librarian
Federal Documents Section
Hawaii State Library
Honolulu, HI

It may have as much to do with a songwriter's choice of color as anything else. This question was addressed years ago. Two songs seem to have had a major influence in establishing the custom. One is an old Irish song, "She Wore a Yellow Ribbon," made popular after World War II when a John Wayne movie took its title from it. The other is the Tony Orlando and Dawn song, "Tie a Yellow Ribbon Round the Old Oak Tree."

I don't know whether or not the custom of wearing a yellow ribbon was really followed by lovers of soldiers in the U.S. Cavalry in the nineteenth century, as postulated in the movie, or whether it was simply a 1950s screenwriter's delight.

The second song was written about a man coming out of prison, but got picked up first during the Iran hostage crisis and then copycatted during the Gulf War. Again, I betcha if the song had said "tie a purple ribbon" we might have seen a proliferation of that colored ribbon instead.

Yellow, according to *Man, Myth and Magic,* is symbolically ambivalent and can represent many things. As the color of cowardice, jealousy, hate, and vindictiveness, it is not an obvious color choice for heroic gestures. But as a color representing the sun, it can also mean perfection, wealth, glory, and power; good things all, but none directly related to the military or remembrance.

John Henderson
Reference Librarian
Ithaca College Library
Ithaca, NY

 "Screenwriter's delight" is too kind! It is probably the number one peeve of U.S. West military historians. Early in the nineteenth century the U.S. Army adopted a color scheme to identify branches of the service: yellow for cavalry, blue for infantry, and red for artillery were the principal ones. (These choices of colors happen to be common to many countries, but I don't know who started the convention.) In the U.S. Army, these colors were most evident in NCOs' sleeve chevrons and the background of officers' shoulder rank insignia. Around 1870, the U.S. Army introduced a full dress based on the victorious Germans in the Franco-Prussian War (complete with spiked helmets). This full dress continued the previous color conventions, but was seldom seen on the frontier. In campaign dress, cavalry yellow was even less evident. The cavalry absolutely never wore yellow kerchiefs as depicted by Hollywood (nor did they have yellow trouser stripes), and I believe it was the non existent yellow kerchiefs that served as the inspiration for the equally nonexistent women's yellow ribbons. In the nineteenth century I would expect that yellow ribbons would have had connotations of cowardice too strong to have been used as Hollywood suggests.

T. F. Mills
Serials Librarian
University of Denver Library
Denver, CO

□　□　□

On the Fringe

 Greetings to all, and I have a backwards question for you.

In this section we receive telephone calls about the gold fringe on the American flag indicating that in that room the Constitution is no longer in effect and that people fall under maritime/admiralty law. We have found no source to support this belief.

I remember last year the question of the gold fringe on the flag arose, and a search under "flag" or "gold fringe" in the Archives brought up a little, most of which I had remembered. Every indication is that the gold fringe is merely an optional decoration, not used too much outside due to weathering and damage from the wind.

This week we had a case of a militia member being arrested for carrying a pistol. According to a report by Linda Hosek in Wednesday's *Honolulu Star-Bulletin,* the militia member refused to enter the courtroom unless he was physically dragged in. The report states:

> ... David Miller, a self-described mainland expert on legal procedure, said Stefanov didn't enter the courtroom because he would have been entering a war zone and would have no rights.
>
> Miller said the fact that the courtroom's flag had gold fringe made it an admiralty flag, where defendants are guilty until proven innocent. . . .

We have already received calls to confirm this statement, but can't find anything. We have looked in the U.S. Code, Titles 4 and 10, and cannot find "gold fringe" mentioned anywhere. Does anyone have any idea where this idea came from, so that we can locate it and have it handy for our patrons to read? For now they seem to feel we are just part of the cover-up of this conspiracy by the government.

Charles King
Reference Librarian
Federal Documents Section
Hawaii State Library
Honolulu, HI

 I forwarded this question to Charles Spain, who was instrumental in rewriting the Texas Flag Code to undercut the silly gold fringe obstructionists. Here is his reply:

Various white supremacist and paramilitary groups allegedly subscribe to the bizarre theory that a fringed U.S. flag in a courtroom means that it is a court martial and not a civil common-law court. I'm not sure these groups actually believe this crap, but they object to the court's jurisdiction nonetheless and waste valuable time.

Their argument is that since the federal civil laws governing the design of the U.S. flag don't authorize the use of fringe (see Title 4, United States Code, sections 1 & 2 and Presidential Executive Order No. 10,834 (21 Aug 59)), but army and naval regulations do authorize the use of fringe on the flag, therefore any fringed U.S. flag must be a military flag (and any courtroom with such a fringed flag must be a court martial). Hopefully anyone who has progressed past elementary school will spot the illogic.

There is a 1925 Attorney General Opinion (34 Op. Att'y Gen. 483) that discusses the propriety of using fringe on military colors and standards. The opinion concludes that fringe does not constitute an integral part of the flag's design and that the use of fringe on military flags does not contravene the law concerning the flag's design passed by Congress, which is silent on the fringe matter. The opinion goes on to say that the president as commander in chief may issue orders authorizing the use of fringe on military colors and standards if the president chooses to do so.

These white supremacist and paramilitary groups use this attorney general opinion to argue that fringed flags in courtrooms are there on the order of the president acting in his capacity as commander in chief, i.e., it's a court martial. These folks are crazy, but they aren't completely stupid!

Well there you have it. It's nonsense, but it's a problem. When I drafted the 1993 revisions to the Texas Flag Code, I intentionally said it was OK to put fringe on the Texas flag to shortcircuit this argument. Not sure I've saved Western Civilization, but one does what one can!

Dr. Whitney Smith and I have been talking about this for a couple of years, and he is interested in any newspaper stories you can send him. His address is Flag Research Center, P.O. Box 580, Winchester, Massachusetts 01890.

T. F. Mills
Serials Librarian
University of Denver Library
Denver, CO

The Congressional Research Service (CRS) has published a report titled *The United States Flag: Federal Law Relating to Display and Associated Questions* CRS Report No. 90-338A (June 30, 1990).

If your library subscribes to any CIS microfiche services, you may have a copy of this in your collection.

On page 12 of same is a section titled *"Ornaments on Flag Staffs, Fringes on Flag."* To summarize, "The placing of fringe on the flag is optional . . . and no Act of Congress or Executive Order either requires or prohibits the practice. . . . The fringe on a flag is considered an 'honorable enrichment only' and its official use by the Army dates from 1865."

The CRS got this information from the Institute of Heraldry, U.S. Army, Bldg. 15, Cameron Station, Alexandria, Virginia 22304-5050.

Also cited was an opinion of the attorney general from 1925 that may be available at a large law library as 34 Op. Atty. Gen. 483 (1925).

As for invoking admiralty jurisdiction, I seriously doubt that this one item could do that; in my opinion the court would have to be moved from its equity sitting to the admiralty sitting.

Chuck Petras
Cleveland, OH

Where the Flag Never Comes Down

Q Patron says that there are five places where the United States flag "never flies at half mast." He thinks four of the five places are

1. *Arizona* Memorial

2. Moon

3. Arlington National Cemetery

4. Fort McHenry

Patron is looking for verification of the answer. By the way, patron is not "exactly sure" if Fort McHenry is one of the four places.

Stuart Schaeffer
Farmingdale Public Library
Farmingdale, NY

 According to Mary Jane McCaffree and Pauline Innis, *Protocol: The Complete Handbook of Diplomatic, Official, and Social Usage:*

Presidential Proclamation 3044 prescribes rules for displaying the flag at half staff on federal property. This proclamation was directed to federal agencies, but the preamble indicates that it was intended also "as a guide to the people of the Nation generally." Federal property for the purpose of this statute includes "all buildings, grounds, and naval vessels of the Federal Government in the District of Columbia and throughout the United States and its territories and possessions . . . all United States Embassies, legations, and other facilities abroad, including all military facilities and naval vessels and stations."

I did not see any exemptions noted, though of the places you mention, the moon certainly does not fall under the category of federal property, and lowering the flag on the moon would be difficult anyhow.

Your patron may be thinking of places that display the flag twenty-four hours a day. Although it is legal to display the flag anywhere for twenty-four hours of the day if properly illuminated, the following places are especially authorized to do so by special laws and proclamations:

1. Fort McHenry (Baltimore, MD)

2. Flag House Square (Baltimore, MD)

3. Battle Green (Lexington, MA)

4. The White House (Washington, DC)

5. Washington Monument (Washington, DC)

6. United States Customs Ports of Entry

7. United States Marine Corps (Iwo Jima) Memorial (Arlington, VA)

8. Valley Forge State Park (Valley Forge, PA)

McCaffree and Innis go on to list some twenty or so places that "customarily" display the flag twenty-four hours a day.

K. Lesley Knieriem
YA/Reference Librarian
South Huntington Public Library
Huntington Station, NY

Bear with the Guards

While watching Queen Elizabeth's birthday celebration my daughter asked me why the Guards wear bearskins hats and if they are still made out of real bearskin. I tried the Web page for the royal family and the British army— nothing. Help! If anyone knows the answer, Stumpers will.

Eileen Moore
Adjunct Instructor, History Department
University of Alabama at Birmingham
Birmingham, AL

Yes, bearskins are real—from Canadian black bears. Other things have gone the cheap route, like plastic belts instead of leather ones, for ease of maintenance. But the army has not yet found an acceptable synthetic substitute for bearskins, and they are too deeply rooted in tradition to give up. No new ones have been made for some time, but army reductions have ensured that there is no severe shortage of gear. The style has remained virtually unchanged since the mid-nineteenth century. They are treated with extreme care, and any guardsman found spiffing his up with chemicals or shoe polish is subject to severe discipline.

Bearskins have been through a long evolution. In Europe in the late seventeenth century, specialist elite troops called grenadiers started wearing brimless caps—probably to facilitate the throwing of grenades without losing their hats. Typically, these hats looked like nightcap stockings with a stiff decorated front panel. The panels evolved into metal plates, and the back of the cap was often decorated with a tuft of bearskin fur. By 1700 in some armies the fur had obscured the whole of the cap except the front panel. The fur was probably an added symbol of the virility of these troops. Since the grenadier caps were associated with elite troops, royal guards regiments also adopted them. In the eighteenth century, most armies, including the British, had a grenadier company in every regiment, and they all wore variations of this grenadier cap.

In 1800 the British Army adopted the shako (a peaked stovepipe hat), and dispensed with tricornes and grenadier caps. But in 1815 the First Regiment of Guards defeated the grenadiers of Napoleon's Imperial Guard at Waterloo, and were shortly afterwards given the new title Grenadier Guards and the right to wear the bearskin of their defeated counterparts. It was similar to the bearskin worn by British guards today. There was probably considerable pressure to do this, since bearskins had remained a guards symbol in much of the rest of Europe. In 1831 the third Guards were renamed the Scots Fusilier Guards and also given the right to wear the bearskin. The only other regiment, the second, or Coldstream Guards, adopted it sometime around 1850. Two more regiments of guards, Irish and Welsh, were formed in 1900 and 1915, by which time the modern-style bearskin was traditional guards headgear. The five regiments of guards can be distinguished from each other by the plumes on their bearskins: Grenadier = white plume on left; Coldstream = red plume on right; Scots = no plume; Irish = "St. Patrick's blue" (i.e., greenish) plume on right; Welsh = white/green/white plume on left.

T. F. Mills
Serials Librarian
University of Denver Library
Denver, CO

 To add just a bit . . . At a distance, the metal plates on the front of the older style of cap to which Mr. Mills refers catch the sun and look like faces. So a rank of troops far away would seem like giants to someone observing them across a battlefield.

The bearskins served much the same purpose—a five-and-a-half-foot soldier became a foot taller. Grenadiers, who were shock troops, favored the bigger, meaner look afforded by more aggressive headgear.

Ross Holt
Head of Reference
Randolph County Public Library
Asheboro, NC

 To add just a bit more to the bearskin hats question for the sake of accuracy (I have checked a few sources since my last off-the-cuff remarks):

The British practice of covering grenadier caps with fur seems to have originated unofficially in the later stages of the French and Indian War (inspired no doubt by a plentiful supply of bears and frontiersmen who dressed themselves liberally in furs). By 1766 bearskin caps for grenadiers were official throughout the army. These were smaller than today's bearskins, had a plate on the front, a grenade badge on the back, and were draped with cords. All these frills on the bearskin were eliminated in 1829 after several minor modifications in design.

When the British Army converted to the shako in 1800, the grenadier companies actually kept their bearskins for parade dress only, and still had them in 1815 when the whole Grenadier Guards regiment converted to them. The Coldstream Guards adopted bearskins sometime between 1815 and 1831 (and not after 1831 as I previously reported). I'm pretty sure the Crimean War was the last time bearskins were worn in battle.

Ross Holt is correct that one function of grenadier caps was to add stature to the soldiers (and made them more intimidating)—but in many cases these shock troops were already giants. The Prussian grenadiers were legendary in this respect. British guards regiments still maintain a six-foot eligibility requirement.

T. F. Mills
Serials Librarian
University of Denver Library
Denver, CO

19 Education

Not Good Enough for Harvard

 An article written about Carl Sagan in a local paper as part of a feature on Cornell University's celebration of his sixtieth birthday happened to mention that he had been denied tenure by Harvard University. That, of course, led several of us to wonder what other prominent scholars, scientists, and personalities have been denied tenure. We have not been able to locate a list. Does anyone know of such a list?

John Henderson
Reference Librarian
Ithaca College Library
Ithaca, NY

 I have never seen a list that would be comprehensive, but City University of New York lore has it that the famous Dr. Ruth was denied tenure at Lehman College.

Danise G. Hoover
Head of Reference
Hunter College Library
New York, NY

A I came across an interesting query posted by John Henderson in 1994, asking for names of famous people who were denied tenure. There were few responses, so I decided to search Nexis for the phrase "denied tenure" to come up with some more names. Here is what I found, including the name of the college said to have denied the person tenure:

novelist Erich Segal (Yale)
artist Roy Lichtenstein (Ohio State)

sociologist Paul Starr (Harvard)

sociologist Theda Skocpol (Harvard)

sociologist Andrew Greeley (University of Chicago)

House Speaker Newt Gingrich (West Georgia College)

novelist Marilyn French (Hofstra)

Nobel Prize–winning economist Paul Samuelson (Harvard)

Supreme Court Justice Ruth Bader Ginsburg (Harvard)

birth control pill inventor Gregory Pincus (Harvard)

Nobel Prize–winning economist Lawrence Klein (University of Michigan)

Fred R. Shapiro
Associate Librarian for Public Services
Yale Law School
New Haven, CT

□ □ □

Only a Few Left

 A patron heard on the radio, possibly G. Gordon Liddy's show, that there are only three all-male colleges left in the United States. Two are the Citadel and VMI. Patron wants to know what the third is. We are undergoing renovations, and most of our collection is under plastic and about a ton of fiberglass insulation. This makes searching a tad difficult.

Stephen Newton
New Castle, DE

The College Board's *College Handbook 1995* lists many more than three colleges for men only. Most of them are seminaries. The others, besides the Citadel and VMI, are Deep Springs College (California), Morehouse College (Georgia), St. Meinrad College (Indiana), Wabash College (Indiana), Divine Word College (Iowa), St. John's University (Minnesota), Hobart College (New York), Williamson

Free School of Mechanical Trades (Pennsylvania), and
Hampden–Sydney College (Virginia).

Rhea Nagle
Information Center
National Association of Colleges and Employers
Bethlehem, PA

 Maybe it's still "in the mail" but I keep expecting to see
someone remark that the Citadel is now off the list of "all-
male" schools. I saw a newspaper article on Sunday stating
that the first female cadet will enter as a cadet this fall,
following the lengthy court battle in which the school
resisted accepting a female student. She has been a day
student for the past year but will now live on campus and
become a "cadet." The AP article is headlined "Citadel
grudgingly makes room for first female cadet," *San Diego
Union-Tribune,* August 6, 1995.

Judy Swink
Resource Librarian
Serra Cooperative Library System
San Diego, CA

Millennial Misconception

 Steve Johnston, a columnist for the *Seattle Times,* fields questions and writes humorous answers in his column twice a week. This one stumped him recently:

When does the twenty-first century start? One reader is sure it doesn't start until the first second of January 1, 2001 and that the year 2000 is part of the twentieth century. In the same vein, if these are the 1990s and the previous decade was the 1980s, what are we going to call the first decade of the twenty-first century? The zeros? The aughts? The naughties?

Our usual sources couldn't answer this question. If you can, please do so.

Katherine Long and Steve Johnston
Reporters
Seattle Times
Seattle, WA

 There never was a year 0. Thus the first year ended on December 31, 01, the first decade on December 31, 10, and the first century on Dec. 31,100. The twentieth century will therefore end on December 30, 2000, and the twenty-first century will not begin until the first second of January 1, 2001. That's the long and short of it as far as facts go. But try convincing people! It sounds so much better to say the new millennium begins on January 1, 2000, and a lot of people, books, and organizations say it does—math and the calendar notwithstanding.

I guess the upside of this is that we can celebrate it twice!

Doug Weller
Langley Junior and Infant School
Solihull, UK

Just a small addition to the discussion on the end of the twentieth century and the beginning of the twenty-first century. While I am in complete agreement with the academic view that the twenty-first century will begin on January 1, 2001, for the usual numerical reasons (numbering systems tend to start at 1 and proceed from there) I am prepared to accept that popular weight of opinion will be celebrating the end of the twentieth century on December 31, 1999, and the voice of the academic will hardly be heard over the voice of Dick Clark announcing the descent of the glittering ball in Times Square.

Jack Corse
Reference Librarian
Simon Fraser University
Burnaby, British Columbia
Canada

 There was no year 0 because only a few cultures had discovered the concept of 0 at the time our calendar was created, and the cultures that created the calendar (Roman, Greek, Egyptian, Hebrew, Babylonian) were *not* among those (basically the Chinese and the Mayans) that knew about 0.

In fact, our (A.D. or C.E.) numbering of years did not begin until what we call the fourth or fifth century, and yes, the person who created it was off by a few years (Jesus was probably born in 4 to 6 B.C., which means the two thousandth anniversary of His birth falls somewhere around now. Odds are really long against December 25th being His real birthday, but no one really knows. If the Herod story in Matthew is true, He had to be born before Herod died, which was in 4 B.C.; if the Luke story is true, it was probably in the spring, because that's when shepherds would have been out in the fields with the flocks all night . . .)

But the Romans, Greeks, etc. did not know about zero (remember, they used letters of their alphabet to represent numbers) and so they counted a year one before the birth of Christ and a year one after . . . so centuries run 1–100, 101–200, 201–300, etc.

As for the millennium, ditto 1–1000, 1001–2000, 2001–3000 . . . Arthur C. Clarke had the right idea. Those of us who know better can celebrate the real millennium a year after everybody else.

What do you call the decade with years beginning in 0? Well, last time we had "the turn of the century," and people referred to the years as "oh-one" or "aught-seven." I suspect people will refer to the coming decade as "the zeros" because our culture is more used to that term now (and maybe because it's going downhill, but that's another story) or maybe "the ohs" (my fiftieth birthday will be 11/18/00, as in "oh-oh!"—which is why I've decided to stay thirty-nine).

Lois Aleta Fundis
Reference Librarian
Mary H. Weir Public Library
Weirton, WV

 The question has occasionally come up about when to celebrate the dawn of the new century. The consensus on Stumpers would seem to be that although it's wrong, there's nothing that can be done to stop most of the world celebrating on January 1, 2000 (instead of 2001).

Now Ruth S. Freitag of the Library of Congress has published a fifty-seven-page bibliography, *The Battle of the*

Centuries, documenting the empirical evidence that centuries begin in the year "one" and how the planet handled it in 1700/01, 1800/01, 1900/01. While there were pockets of "impressively convoluted" resistance to the idea of celebrating in 1901, historically most people have celebrated the dawn of a new century at the correct time.

It seems the digit "2" for the new millennium will throw off most people for the first time in modern history. Even if they have it all wrong, I'd love to be at the World Millennium Ball which starts at 6 P.M. GMT on December 31, 1999, at the Great Pyramid.

T. F. Mills
Serials Librarian
University of Denver Library
Denver, CO

□   □   □

Naughty Aughties

Q Does anyone know if there is a name for the first decade of a century? For example, there are the thirties, forties, etc. I have looked in various thesauruses and specialized dictionaries and have also perused books on the turn of the century, but I have not come across any definitive word.

Susan Browning
Resource Specialist 2
Metro Transit
Houston, TX

A SCAN (Southern California Answer Network) worked on this question in 1993 and reported its findings in its newsletter *SCAN/INFO,* February 1993, which in turn included a humorous reprint of an article from the *New York Times,* December 30, 1992, p. 12. The upshot of all this is that there appears to be no definitive answer. We could call them "oughties," "the 00's" (pronounced "ohs"), or even the "naughties," since *naught* is sometimes used for *ought*. In *Quoth the Maven* (pp. 184–88) William Safire suggests holding off until 2009, when we will know whether we are either in prosperity or depression, and then deciding what to call the whole decade.

Rosy Brewer
Reference Librarian
Monterey Bay Cooperative Library System (MOBAC)
Monterey, CA

□ □ □

2001: A Pronunciation Odyssey

 Will we stop using the "two thousand" pronunciation after a few years into the twenty-first century?

Someone said the American Association for the Advancement of Science's educational reform effort, Project 2061, has been pronounced "twenty sixty-one," not "two-thousand sixty-one," since at least 1988.

So what will be the correct way of saying 2004, 2018, etc. . . . ?

Dawn Marie Simpson
Marketing Coordinator
Westinghouse Power Generation Business Unit
Orlando, FL

 My *guess* is that we will switch when we reach 2010 (twenty-ten); twenty-nine etc. doesn't quite work, but we've all been singing "In the year twenty-five twenty-five" for years and have heard many such variations of twenty- . . . . However, the movie was pronounced "Two Thousand One: A Space Odyssey." So I feel the probable answer will be "two thousand one; two thousand two . . . two thousand nine; twenty-ten."

Judy Swink
Resource Librarian
Serra Cooperative Library System
San Diego, CA

Perhaps the first nine years of the century will be pronounced as they often were for the first nine years of the present century:

20 aught 1, 20 aught 2, 20 aught 3, etc.

More probably, people will do in 2001 what they do now for the first part of the twentieth century:

19 oh 1, 19 oh 2, 19 oh 3, etc.

That's my best guess. I think what many people stumble over is the presence of two zeros.

David K. Barnhart
Editor
Barnhart Dictionary Companion
Cold Spring, NY

☐ ☐ ☐

125th Puzzler

 Does anyone know the Latin-derived term for a 125th anniversary?

Burlington Public Library
Burlington, IA

 Our quick reference file shows *quasquicentennial* for the 125th anniversary, which I verified in the *Random House Dictionary of the English Language*—like so many things, it's easy to find when you already know the answer!

Sarah Caltvedt
Glen Ellyn Public Library
Glen Ellyn, IL

□ □ □

175th Puzzler

Q I hope some people out there may have this in ready reference, or even in their head! We are trying to figure out what
the 175th anniversary of an event would be called (as with
the 100th being the *centennial* or the 150th being the
sesquicentennial). Have looked in almanacs, *New York
Public Library Desk Reference,* and Latin grammars
without success.

Bill Lowe
Reference Librarian
Westminster College
Fulton, MO

A At last! There was discussion here a few months ago
about a word for the 175th anniversary. I responded
that *quasquicentennial* has become established for 125th
anniversaries, but I could find no evidence of a word
for 175th. Well, in tomorrow's "On Language" column
by William Safire in the *New York Times* magazine
section (wombats know Sunday's newspaper on Saturday), Safire reports that Robert L. Chapman, the lexi-
cographer who coined *quasquicentennial* over thirty years
ago, now suggests *terquasquicentennial* for a 175th anniversary.

Fred R. Shapiro
Associate Librarian for Public Services
Yale Law School
New Haven, CT

□ □ □

Thirty Mnemonics Hath September

Q On the COPYEDIT-L list we have been discussing variants
of "Thirty days hath September . . ."

Three typical versions:

Thirty days hath September,
April, June, and November.
All the rest have thirty-one,
Excepting February alone,
Which has twenty-eight days clear,
And twenty-nine in each leap year.

Thirty days hath September,
April, June and November.
All the rest have 31,
except for February, which alone,
has 28 and one day more
in each and every year of four.

Thirty days hath September,
April, June, and November
All the rest have Strawberry Jam
Except for grandma alone
And she rides a bike.

I don't know of an equivalent of the Opies' work for school mnemonics. Does anybody know of such a work, or the earliest date and form of this rhyme?

David Ibbetson
Toronto, Ontario
Canada

 The Annotated Mother Goose by William S. Baring-Gould and Cecil Baring-Gould lists this as poem 328 (the first version above, with minor wording variation). The footnote is too long to reproduce here; if you don't have access to a copy, let me know and I will get same to you. (It notes that "the rhyme goes back at least to an old play of 1606, *The Return from Parnassus.*") It also lists a couple of other school mnemonics.

I recall an exchange of letters in *Mad* magazine sometime in the mid- or late 1950s that added a couple of joke versions; and I have always remembered the version the letter column editor gave as his favorite, which is a variant of your last one:

> *Thirty days hath September,*
> *April, June, and no wonder,*
> *All the rest have peanut butter,*
> *Except my grandmother—*
> *She has a little red tricycle.*

While I'm at it, I might note that I have never seen or heard anywhere else the mnemonic my father taught me for the presidents of the United States:

We Are Just Making Money At Just Valuation. Here, Tommy, Please Take Five Pence, But Leave Jane—Good, Honest Girl—A Cool Hundred.

It will be noticed that this takes us up only to Benjamin Harrison, stuck in the middle of Grover Cleveland I and Grover Cleveland II: The Revenge. Presumably when my father was a school kid everything thereafter was considered such recent history as not to need a mnemonic. But I am wondering if anyone else has ever seen or heard this one, or even a longer and more up-to-date version?

Dennis Lien
Reference Librarian
Wilson Library
University of Minnesota
Minneapolis, MN

 OK, here are the presidents:

Washington and Jefferson made many a joke;

Van Buren had to put the frying pan back;

Lincoln just gasped, "Heaven guard America!"

Cleveland had coats made ready to wear home.

Coolidge hurried right to every kitchen jar nook.

Ford cut right brow.

Not great—but it works! Of course, I think a rhyme would work much better—and I'm sure there's some enterprising wombat out there composing one as we speak.

Sally G. Waters
Queen of Reference
Stetson College of Law Library
St. Petersburg, FL

21 The Body

Role Model?

 Is there a documented source for this information: If Barbie were a real woman, based on her dimensions, she would be something like seven feet tall! Also, are there articles or books exploring the negative impact of Barbie on girls?

 Dimensions? If people had started with Barbie's brain size, they might not have gotten into trouble with emulating her other "endowments."

Jo Falcon mentions a few:

M. G. Lord (who used to cross-dress her Ken), *Forever Barbie: The Unauthorized Biography of a Real Doll.*

With specific reference to your question, check out chapter 12, "The Women Who Would Be Barbie," about a fan who's had $55,000 worth of cosmetic surgery to emulate the doll.

The person was Cindy Jackson, subject of an episode of *The Jerry Springer Show,* first broadcast March 15, 1993, available on video from Multimedia Entertainment.

Another article that I don't think has been mentioned:

Kamy Cunningham, "Barbie Doll Culture and the American Waistland," *Symbolic Interaction,* spring 1993, vol. 16, no. 1, p. 79.

Some theses that should be available through Interlibrary Loan:

Ware, Sally Elizabeth. *Looking at Barbie: Social Comparison Processes and Body Esteem Among Women.* MA, U of Nebraska, 1991.

Gordon, Sharon. *From "Barbie" to "He-Man": A Review of Feminist Theories of Gender Theory and Their Application for Early Childhood Education.* MSEd, Bank Street College of Ed, 1987.

Sharp, Shannon. *Barbie as an Influential Factor in Adolescent Eating Disorders.* BS, Cal Poly, 1994.

What do you call a Barbie with half a brain? Gifted.

What do you call it when Barbie dyes her hair? Artificial intelligence.

What do Barbie and a beer bottle have in common? Both are empty from the neck up.

How do you measure Barbie's IQ? With a tire gauge.

Why does Barbie wash her hair in the sink? Because that's where you wash vegetables.

How do you make Barbie's eyes sparkle? Shine a flashlight in her ear.

T. F. Mills
Serials Librarian
University of Denver Library
Denver, CO

 In today's *Portland Oregonian,* August 28, 1996, Living section, p. 1, is an article reporting that a team of Australian researchers computed the neck, chest, arm, waist, hip, thigh, calf, and ankle measurements of Barbie—based on her being of average height (which wasn't given in this article). According to the article, Barbie's "key measurements" would be 36-18-33, which means that the probability of meeting a woman with the same measurements is less than 1 in 100,000. Ken is more realistic at 1 in 50. Source: Kevin Norton of the University of South Australia.

Janet Irwin
Reference Librarian
Multnomah County Library
Portland, OR

□   □   □

A Bargain at Twice the Price

 We have a patron who is looking for the (approximate) dollar value of the elements that are found in the human body. This is something many of us remember hearing of in chemistry classes or the like and think is a fairly low figure. The patron is preparing a speech on human worth and would like to use it as an illustration. We have checked almanacs, encyclopedias, trivia books, and chemistry and anatomy references with no luck.

Martha Sink
Librarian
Central North Carolina Regional Library
Burlington, NC

 We too have had this question. In the *U.S. News & World Report* of July 23, 1979, p. 6, a short article states that the elements of the body were worth $6.50 in 1979 dollars. The article also reports that in 1956 the body's value was $0.98. The source for the article was the Monsanto Corp. Wish this was more current, but it's the latest we've found.

The *New York Public Library Book of Answers,* p. 102, has a discussion that takes a slightly different approach. It cites an unnamed doctor as stating that the body is worth "at least $169,834—not counting $1,200 worth of blood." The doctor is no doubt placing a value on body parts, rather than the elements.

Philip Jones
Head, Reference Services Department
Central Arkansas Library System
Little Rock, AR

 I thought I would post this info for all interested. I have been looking for the answer off and on for at least a year and at first there was nothing at all in the Archives. What is there now is fairly old information. Within the last two weeks (thanks to some Web and EBSCO searching) I have come up with a much more current figure for what the (chemical) elements of the average human body are worth in U.S. dollars.

According to the American Chemical Society (as reported in *Popular Science,* May 1993, p. 24), the real value of the body's chemicals is about $1.25, but the potential value (hormones, etc.) is in millions of dollars. Expanding on the theme, the organization also sells a T-shirt with the following logo: "Raw Materials = $25.00, Finished Product = $6 million (assembly required)."

I was not given any details on the "raw materials" figure, but I would suppose that includes things like plasma, etc. (?)

Becky Wurm Clark
Reference Library Assistant III
Lincoln City Libraries
Lincoln, NE

 It depends what you mean by "elements." If you really mean Elements, then you are talking about Carbon and Oxygen and Nitrogen and Hydrogen, a little Iron and Calcium, and little else. That's not worth much. (And I don't mean hardly anything else, I mean hardly any of a whole bunch of other stuff.)

But as you have pointed out, put things together and things get more valuable (relationship is the key). Then you get compounds and molecules like water and as you get more relational, you get plasma, blood, proteins, hormones, cells, muscles, organs, systems. It's the relationship that makes that stuff valuable—not the elemental components. I know that gold is valuable as an element, but carbon is dirt cheap and diamonds are worth far more than gold. Unless you are building a computer circuit. Then diamond is worthless and gold is valuable. But not as valuable as silicon. But not sand. And not glass either.

And I don't mean simple supply and demand. But this starts me off on a discourse about mechanism and digital worldviews versus relational and analogical ones . . . and I've already had my hand spanked today.

Warren Heitzenrater
Durham, NC

 If the premise of Arthur Porges's short story "$1.98" (May 1954 issue of *Magazine of Fantasy and Science Fiction*) is correct, the value of the human body as of late 1953/early 1954 was $1.98—per an unspecified newspaper article mentioned in the story.

The story involves a lovesick young man who does a favor for a very minor genie, whose powers are so limited that he cannot grant a wish for any merchandise of value above $1.98. The solution is about what you would expect, and is not very politically correct even for the 1950s, I would have thought. . . .

Dennis Lien
Reference Librarian
Wilson Library
University of Minnesota
Minneapolis, MN

Nuke Them Roaches

 This morning a patron told me that he had read a magazine article within the last year stating that some scientist with nothing better to do had been feeding nuclear waste products to cockroaches, and that lo and behold, the rumors about cockroaches were true and the bugs were thriving. I was unable to find the article in Nexis, but I did confirm that the belief in the immunity of cockroaches to atomic weaponry seems to be a well-established urban legend. My question is, does anyone know of any actual research that has been done to back up this theory? Perhaps observations made after Hiroshima?

Hailey Leithauser
Reference Librarian
U.S. Department of Energy
Washington, DC

 I can provide some verification from personal experience. During my first year of graduate school I was assigned the prime dorm room directly over the rubbish tip; as a result I was flooded with the disgusting little vermin. I'll spare you the saga of my yearlong and ultimately futile battle with the critters, but on one memorable occasion I was about to microwave my supper when a roach crawled into the oven. I immediately slammed the door shut and nuked that sucker on high for five minutes; but when I opened the door, the little pest emerged with nary an antenna out of place.

K. Lesley Knierem
YA/Reference Librarian
South Huntington Public Library
Huntington Station, NY

A bit of background may help here: we may call them "nukes," but the radiation used is anything but nuclear. It is ordinary radio waves, of the sort used in radar. The heating effect is due to the slight differences between radio and infrared frequencies, both being fairly close together on the low end of the spectrum. Nuclear radiation is gamma and is entirely on the other end of the spectrum—much, much higher than visible light, and among the most energetic in the universe. The microwave effects were noted first as a result of what happened to birds roosting or nesting in radar antennae . . . some of the older units were megawatters, which could kill the birds in seconds.

The roach survived partly because of luck . . . I zapped a fly the other day, and he died . . . and partly by physics. In a microwave oven the waves enter from a guide in the top or one side, and they propagate by reflection back and forth. In the way of all wave phenemona, this causes nodes of reinforcement and annihilation of the waves, leading to spots where intensity is very low. That's why turntables are used: to even out heating in the foods. The roach, being small, has a high probability of staying in one node of low intensity. The fly, smaller as he is, still has a higher probability of flying into one of high intensity.

As for the widespread public belief in the insect's resistance, that may come from *The Hellstrom Chronicle,* a pseudoscientific movie of thirty years back based on a kernel of truth. The depiction of insects as resistant is actually correct, since their DNA is simpler and thus has a lower probability of suffering "fatal" mutations over generations. Individual insects, however, have a resistance only slightly different from other organisms.

O. H. McKagen
Blacksburg, VA

The reasoning behind the prediction that insects will inherit the earth, survive nuclear war, or outlast all other life has to do with their adaptability, as evidenced by their variety. That adaptability depends, at least in part, on short generations. It's not that insects somehow avoid lethal mutations, but that because each generation is produced so quickly and includes so many individuals, at least a few are likely to possess the genes to survive whatever occurs.

Plenty of insect species have become extinct, but there are still more *kinds* of beetles than there are of every other kind of animal life put together. Rather than a cockroach, I'd put my money on some kind of scavenger beetle as the last living thing on earth. In one of his essays, Stephen J. Gould traces the history of a quotation where a scientist, asked what his studies have taught him about the nature of God, allegedly replies, "He is inordinately fond of beetles."

The general concept of insect survival appears in the writings of several British authors by the beginning of this century, if not earlier.

Carolyn Caywood
Bayside Area Librarian
Virginia Beach, VA

 Actually, ask *any* microbiologist, and you will find that microbes rule this planet, with all of the other lifeforms being merely hosts for them. There are forms of microbiotic life that do not require oxygen or light and can get by with minimal nutrients. Without water they can go into a dormant phase and behave as non living material for many, many years. The microbes let the cockroaches carry them around because they are such efficient hosts.

Montgomery Phair
Reference Librarian
Baltimore County Public Library
Randallstown, MD

The Hellstrom Chronicle (1971) may have helped popularize the idea, but it was clearly around long before then; I recall it as a common fact/legend in various science fiction stories in (I think) the fifties and sixties, and there are many "the future belongs to the insects" stories well before then that do not deal with nuclear radiation, such as *Mad Planet* and *Red Dust* by Murray Leinster, which date from 1920–21.

Dennis Lien
Reference Librarian
Wilson Library
University of Minnesota
Minneapolis, MN

A Million Monkeys

 What is the exact quotation to the effect that a large number of monkeys, seated at typewriters, would eventually produce the works of Shakespeare?

 Here is the whole entry from *Respectfully Quoted:*

If I let my fingers wander idly over the keys of a typewriter it *might* happen that my screed made an intelligible sentence. If an army of monkeys were strumming on typewriters they *might* write all the books in the British Museum. Arthur S. Eddington, *The Nature of the Physical World,* chap. 4, p. 72 (1928). Eddington calls this "a rather classical illustration" of chance.

Madeline Schulman
Senior Librarian
Ocean County Library
Toms River, NJ

 The amount of time required is large but *finite*. I haven't bothered to do the calculations, but to produce a single act of Hamlet by this means might well exceed the age of the universe. To simplify matters, assume that the typewriters have 28 keys for the capital letters, space, and new line, that no line can have less than 20 nor more than 100 characters, and that a line ends when the new-line key is reached. Then the number of possible 20-character lines is 27^{20}, the number of possible 21-character lines is 27^{21}, etc. Add all these possibilities together and you have the number of possibilities for each line. This is a *large* number. Then go on from there.

David Ibbetson
Toronto, Ontario
Canada

 This thread brings to mind a contemporary classic quotation: "We've all heard that a million monkeys banging on a million typewriters will eventually reproduce the entire works of Shakespeare. Now, thanks to the Internet, we know this is not true."

Fred R. Shapiro
Associate Librarian for Public Services
Yale Law School
New Haven, CT

The Lion King

 Why is the lion called the king of the jungle when lions don't even live in the jungle?

 As Kate Cummings has pointed out, the lion was known as the king of beasts long before he was dubbed king of the jungle—in fact, two or three thousand years before anybody who wrote for us to read had even seen a jungle. He is so described by Greeks and Romans, and the same implication is in Genesis, where Judah is styled the whelp of a lion. These were clearly lions known from the Middle East, Asia Minor, and North Africa. I suspect that the term "king of the jungle" arose in the nineteenth century, though I have no idea who may have coined it.

John Dyson
Department of Spanish and Portuguese
Indiana University
Bloomington, IN

 John's intuitions are supported by the *Oxford English Dictionary*, which records the English phrase "king of beasts" back to Gower (1390), but does not note "king of the jungle" at all.

Fred R. Shapiro
Associate Librarian for Public Services
Yale Law School
New Haven, CT

 The earliest title using "king of the jungle" that I can find is the 1935 Buster Crabbe movie of that name, an adaptation of *The Lion's Way* by British author C. T. Stoneham. (The book was also reprinted in a *Photoplay* edition under that title.) But I'm sure that Tarzan was referred to many times as "King of the Jungle," "Lord of the Jungle," "Jungle Lord," and such variants. (*The Lion's Way*, incidentally, is very much in the Tarzan and Mowgli tradition: its hero, Kaspa, is raised by lions instead of apes or wolves . . .)

I suspect the idea of lions as living in jungle conditions and of Africa as being virtually one entire jungle end to end precedes Edgar Rice Burroughs, but certainly his works and the spin-offs therefrom popularized the idea. ERB, incidentally, never visited Africa in his life, and there are a fair number of howlers in the stories as a result— notably in the first, magazine version of *Tarzan of the Apes* in which Tarzan, roaming the African jungle, kills a *tiger*. Someone seems to have gently pointed out the obvious problem to ERB, who changed the victim to a lion in the book reprint. Then there's the whole "great apes" thing

(Tarzan's ape buddies are specifically neither chimpanzees nor gorillas, but some otherwise unknown apes somewhere between those two in size and strength).

In spite of all this, and more, I admit to a fondness for Burroughs, and recommend the book *Tarzan and Tradition: Classical Myth in Popular Literature* by Erling B. Holtsmark to all those who want to justify a comparable fondness to themselves or others.

Dennis Lien
Reference Librarian
Wilson Library
University of Minnesota
Minneapolis, MN

Flushing Folklore

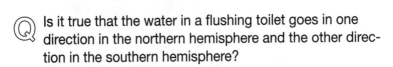 Is it true that the water in a flushing toilet goes in one direction in the northern hemisphere and the other direction in the southern hemisphere?

 It's called the "Coriolis effect" or force (after French mathematician Gaspard Gustave de Coriolis, 1792–1843). *Webster's New World Dictionary* defines it as "an apparent force on a moving object when observed from a rotating system, as the surface of the earth: it is proportional to the speed of the object and is in a direction perpendicular to its direction of motion." You can achieve the same effect by attempting to walk a straight line blindfolded: you will veer from the line to the right or left depending on your hemisphere (and sobriety).

T. F. Mills
Serials Librarian
University of Denver Library
Denver, CO

The standard answer to the question is yes. The phenomenon is called the Coriolis effect.

The problem is that it is a very small effect, and in toilet bowls and bathtubs local imperfections in the tub or bowl, the direction of the water when it is poured into the tub/bowl, and residual currents are likely to supersede the Coriolis effect, especially in a toilet where the water has no time to calm down.

Even Flood
Reference Librarian
Norwegian DIANE Center
Technical University Library of Norway
Trondheim, Norway

Actually, the direction of rotation of the vortex in a flushed toilet bowl depends more on the peculiarities of the bowl's design and the disturbances of flow of the inrushing and outrushing water.

It is a popular belief that whirlpools, vortices, tornadoes, etc. rotate one way in the northern hemisphere and the other in the southern. However, this really isn't true. Some "experts" have stated that the Coriolis force causes this phenomenon, and perhaps that would be true in the absence of all other influences. However, in many cases other factors are at work. A local disturbance, something as simple as a large rock underwater or a cliff face in the air, has far more effect on the direction of rotation. Hence, observed phenomena in both hemispheres rotate in both directions.

To test this: Fill a bathtub with water. Pull out the stopper, and observe the direction of rotation of the resulting whirlpool. Repeat several times. Chances are, you will observe both rotations. The slight disturbance caused by pulling the plug is enough variation to cause this result. If not, try swirling your hand in the water in the opposite direction as it goes down, and you will find that the rotation is easily reversed.

Gary Lee Phillips
Computer Services Librarian
Columbia College
Chicago, IL

 We have in our collection a book by Ira Flatow titled *Rainbows, Curve Balls and Other Wonders of the Natural World Explained,* which includes a chapter on the Coriolis force ("Tornado in the Drain"). Flatow mainly discusses water draining in a tub or sink, but says of toilets, "Even though the toilet flushes in a vortex, the swirl is caused by jets of water cleaning the bowl."

Maureen Derenzy
Director
Otsego County Library
Gaylord, MI

Century Plant

 I have someone who would like to know the name of the plant at the Oxford Library that recently bloomed for the first time in five hundred years.

Mary Morris
Reference Librarian
Macon State College Library
Macon, GA

 Could this be the horticultural rarity you're looking for? The following article may be a lead:

A rare South American Century Plant bloomed in Britain for the first time in 99 years after air conditioning broke down in a greenhouse at Oxford University's botanical gardens and the temperature soared, botanists said Friday.

The plant last blossomed in 1896, shortly after it was acquired by Oxford. As the temperature rose, the 3-foot high plant grew a 12-foot high spike that flowered into hundreds of tiny blossoms.

"Bloom of the Century," *New York Times,* June 13, 1995, section A, p. 10, col. 4.

I'm a horticulturist at heart, as are many of my friends and associates. A little over ten years ago, my former graduate school office mate, Barbara Ramirez, theorized that if a plant thinks it's about to die, it will bloom madly because part of the purpose of its blossoming is to continue itself as a biological species. Her theory is that if you subject a plant to life-threatening conditions, i.e., if you scare it out of its wits, it will flower prolifically—like there's no tomorrow.

This theory seems to work with any plant—from African violets to hardy trees and shrubs grown in the garden. The situation with the century plant seems to be the reverse of this theory, however. One would assume that the century plant—an *Agave,* which is a native to hot, arid climes— would have thought it was going to die inside an air-conditioned greenhouse. When the air-conditioning died, the century plant probably thought to itself as the temperature rose higher and higher: "I'm back home in the South American desert! Time to bloom and set fruit before they get that air-conditioning system repaired and chill me out again!"

If you'd like to see a specimen of the century plant's American cousin, *Agave Americana,* you'll find a fine one growing in the walled garden of the Juliet Gordon Low House in Savannah. The *Agave Americana,* or century plant, was very popular among nineteenth-century American horticulturists.

Jay Evatt
Reference Department
University of Georgia Libraries
Athens, GA

24 Technology and Communications

Beeper Man

 Who invented the beeper or pager?

 The question of exactly who invented what is always a matter of controversy and uncertainty. The issue of who invented the steam engine has never been resolved to the satisfaction of some. Rarely is something invented in the kind of public glare that makes it possible to declare definitively that so-and-so invented the whatchamacallit.

In more than one interview with Gloria Swanson, *she* claimed to have invented a precursor of the beeper/pager, and she reiterated that claim in her autobiographical memoir *Swanson on Swanson.* No technical details were given in any of the accounts I've read, however, and I haven't seen any evidence that would substantiate her boast.

The person generally credited with inventing the beeper/pager is Jack Scantlin, an electronic genius, off-the-wall maverick, and not-so-hot manager. He is also given most of the credit for inventing the first successful ATMs.

In subsequent years, Scantlin has been involved in some far-ranging and bizarre ventures.

A 1981 UPI report told of Scantlin's luxurious ski resort in California, where skiers would be transported by helicopters rather than having to wait in line for forty-five minutes to board a ski lift.

In September 1991 a Xinhua News Agency report announced that Scantlin had been ordered deported by the government of Vanuatu, where he had lived since 1987. Scantlin had been involved in trying to establish a worldwide computer link to conduct financial transactions. He was a confidential adviser to Walter Lini, the prime minister of Vanuatu. Then Lini was ousted from his post in a parliamentary no-confidence vote. The rebels who won the no-confidence vote accused Scantlin in Vanuatu's parliament of wanting to set up a "secret" scheme that allegedly posed the danger of being used by money launderers.

Scantlin was described in a 1961 edition of *Newsweek* as a "scientist turned businessman" with a penchant for sports cars and surfing. He also seems to have a penchant for secrecy. For such a fascinating person, very little has been written about him.

Jim Hunt
Associate Professor
Business and Online Search Specialist
University Library
California State University
Dominguez Hills, CA

□ □ □

It's All Been Done

Ⓠ This one has been truly frustrating, as I have seen the quote myself *somewhere* recently but cannot begin to capture when/where!

Patron has asked for the source of a quotation attributed to Charles H. Duell, a former commissioner of patents, to the effect that "everything that can be invented has already been invented." *Great Business Quotations,* p. 178, attributes it to Duell but patron believes he has seen it attributed to President McKinley.

I have searched the Archives and done multiple Web searches with no success. If anyone has something in their files, I'd deeply appreciate knowing of it.

We have searched a large number of quotation dictionaries without finding it again. I have also searched various biographical resources, and learned that Duell's father was commissioner of patents in the 1870s. Charles Duell was commissioner from 1898 (McKinley appointment) until he resigned in 1901. I have looked at the annual reports submitted by both Duells and find nothing like this.

Judy Swink
Resource Librarian
Serra Cooperative Library System
San Diego, CA

 We looked for this in compiling *Respectfully Quoted*. This is as close as we could come:

The advancement of the arts from year to year taxes our credulity, and seems to presage the arrival of that period when human improvement must end.

HENRY L. ELLSWORTH,

U.S. commissioner of patents, *Annual Report*, p. 5 (1843)

Suzy Platt
Information Management Specialist
Library of Congress
Washington, DC

 According to folklorist David P. Mikkelson in the *New York Times*, October 15, 1995:

The origins of this quotation were researched by Dr. Eber Jeffery more than 50 years ago as part of a project conducted under the aegis of the District of Columbia Historical Records Survey. He found no evidence that any official of the United States Patent Office (including Charles H. Duell, to whom the quotation is most often attributed) had ever resigned his post or recommended that the office be closed because he thought there was nothing left to invent.

Fred R. Shapiro
Associate Librarian for Public Services
Yale Law School
New Haven, CT

□ □ □

Area Code Anecdote

Here's an easy one. At least that's what we thought before we tried to find the answer. What is the date that the first (telephone) area codes were used?

I tried the Archives, as well as *several* print sources at the library, and did not find any mention of a date, only lists of area codes.

Roberta Lincoln
Reference Librarian
Rockford Public Library
Rockford, IL

There is a good article on area codes in *Popular Mechanics,* November 1951, p. 128. According to this article, area codes were in use by operators before 1945, but the first public use was by some ten thousand telephone subscribers in Englewood, New Jersey, in the fall of 1951. They were to test it and could dial direct to several cities in the United States, but not just anywhere. The article has a map of the first area code system, and a nice explanation of how it works. I got to the article by using the *Oxford English Dictionary* under the word *area.*

Peter R. Neal
Retired
Former Head of Reference
Durham County Public Library
Durham, NC

Spam Spam Spam

Q I hope I don't get spammed for this, but does anyone know how the term *spamming* was coined for mass e-mailing?

I checked the Internet books that are available in my library, but spamming is not mentioned.

Terry Wirick
Information Services Librarian
Erie County Public Library
Erie, PA

A An explanation that I find plausible cites a Monty Python skit set in a coffee shop where every item on the menu contains Spam. "Egg and Spam; egg, bacon, and Spam; egg, bacon, sausage, and Spam; Spam, egg, sausage, and Spam; egg, bacon, Spam, and sausage; . . ."

As the waitress recites the menu, a group of Vikings, sitting at a table in the background, chant: "Spam, Spam, Spam, Spam, lovely Spam, wonderful Spam. . . ." increasing in volume until they drown out the waitress.

The aptness of the allusion is enhanced by the image of Spam hitting a fan.

Anton Sherwood
San Francisco, CA

□ □ □

Information Superbuzzword

Q Who coined the term *information superhighway?*

It is frequently claimed that Al Gore coined this term in 1979. William Safire (*New York Times,* April 17, 1994) notes that Gore's claim is "without citations." The earliest documented usage appears to be in *Newsweek,* January 3, 1983.

Fred R. Shapiro
Associate Librarian for Public Services
Yale Law School
New Haven, CT

 I seem to recall that in the early 1980s the Germans were using the term *Infobahn* (presumably a compound word, for which the Germans have a predilection, combining *Information* and *Autobahn*). Could Mr. Gore, or *Newsweek,* or someone else have purloined and Anglicized the term? Unfortunately, I have been unable to trace the German origins of *Infobahn.*

James J. Reca
Knoxville, TN

 I believe *Infobahn* was coined by Americans, not Germans, in an attempt to come up with something more concise than *information superhighway.* Its provenance is undoubtedly later than the early 1980s.

Fred R. Shapiro
Associate Librarian for Public Services
Yale Law School
New Haven, CT

☐ ☐ ☐

Net Nativity

 What is the date of the birth of the Internet?

 The exact date depends somewhat on your definition of the Internet, but one commonly accepted date is

December 1969. Here is an excerpt from my Capsule History of the Internet:

The Internet was started in 1969 under a contract let by the Advanced Research Projects Agency (ARPA), which connected four major computers at universities in the southwestern U.S. (UCLA, Stanford Research Institute, UCSB, and the University of Utah). The contract was carried out by BBN of Cambridge, Mass. and went online in December 1969.

Walt Howe
Delphi Forum Manager
Woburn, MA

Index of Topics and Concepts

Entries printed in **boldface** appear as main entries in the text.

Index of Contributors